Collins
English for Work

Workplace English 1
James Schofield

HarperCollins Publishers
77-85 Fulham Palace Road
Hammersmith
London W6 8JB

First edition 2011

Reprint 10 9 8 7 6 5 4 3 2 1

© HarperCollins Publishers 2011

ISBN 978-0-00-743199-1

Collins ® is a registered trademark
of HarperCollins Publishers Limited

www.collinselt.com

A catalogue record for this book is available
from the British Library.

Typeset in India by Aptara

Printed in China

Cameraman: Jamie Turner
Sound engineer: Stuart Thompson
Actors: Charlotte Brimble, Dai Davison,
Lucy Newman-Williams,
Clare Rickard, David Shaw-Parker
Photographs by Toby Madden

Introduction

Welcome to Workplace English 1

This course gives you the English you need to talk to visitors, clients and colleagues while you carry out your day-to-day work.

The 24 units are in four modules: Meeting for the first time, Emails, Telephoning, and Meeting again.

Each unit begins with a conversation for you to read, watch or listen to. The conversations present the key language. Then there are activities for you to practise the key language including speaking exercises. There is an Answer key at the back of the book.

A DVD and an Audio CD are included in the course. The DVD contains the video for Units 1 to 6 and Units 19 to 24.

If you see this symbol ⊙ you need to watch the DVD.

If you see this symbol ◀)) you need to listen to the CD.

We recommend you spend about 45 to 60 minutes on each unit.

In addition, at the back of the book, there are very useful reference sections for you to use and refer to in your day-to-day work.

While you are working through this book, you will see the following symbols after certain words:

(UK) means that the word is more commonly used in British English.
(US) means that the word is more commonly used in American English.

We hope you enjoy using this self-study course. Good luck in your career!

Contents

Resource bank

1   At reception

Greeting visitors | Asking somebody's name | Completing a form

Conversation

DVD

1   Sally Smith is the receptionist at Lowis Engineering in London. John Carter and Paul Rogers are visiting the company today. Read their conversation and watch the video. Who do they want to see?

Sally	**Good morning, how can I help you?**
John	Good morning. We're here to see Diane Kennedy at 10 o'clock.
Sally	**Can I have your names, please?**
John	Yes, it's John Carter and Paul Rogers from Australian Power Utilities. Here's my business card.
Sally	Thank you. **I'll just call Ms Kennedy.**
Paul	Thank you.
Sally	And **can you complete these security forms, please?**
Paul	Of course. Excuse me, can I have a pen?
Sally	Here you are. Diane? I have Mr Rogers and Mr Carter in reception for you. Right. Thank you.
Sally	Thank you. **Please could you wear these visitors' badges? Someone will come down to get you in a moment. Please have a seat.**
Paul	Thanks.
John	OK.

Did you know?

In English we do not use the 24-hour-clock in everyday conversation. If we want to make it clear it is morning or afternoon, we normally use *am* or *pm*, or say *in the morning* or *in the afternoon / evening*.

Understanding

DVD

2 Watch again. Are the sentences true (T) or false (F)?

1 John and Paul work at Lowis Engineering.	T / F
2 Diane knows John and Paul are coming to see her.	T / F
3 John and Paul will have to wear badges.	T / F
4 John and Paul will have to wait a long time for Diane.	T / F

Key phrases

Dealing with visitors at reception

Good morning / afternoon / evening, ...	*Please could you wear this badge / these badges?*
How can I help you?	
Can I have your name(s), please?	*Someone will come down to get you.*
I'll just call Ms	*Please have a seat.*
Can you complete this form / these forms, please?	

Practice

3 Put the words in the sentences into the correct order.

1 evening, Good help I can how you

_____?

2 I Can names, your please have

_____?

3 Please you these complete could forms

_____?

4 will get come Someone down to you

_____.

5 seat Please a have

_____.

4 Match the questions to the answers.

Receptionist	Visitor
1 Good afternoon. How can I help you?	**A** Ali Khan.
2 Could you wear this badge, please?	**B** I'm here to see Diane Kennedy.
3 Can I have your name, please?	**C** Can you give me a pen?
4 Please can you complete this form?	**D** Of course.

5 Look at John Carter's business card and complete the details on the visitor form.

Lowis Engineering – Visitor Form

Surname / Last name _____

First / Given name _____

Company address _____

Email _____

Visiting _____

Time in _____9.30_____ Time out _____

Signature _*John Carter*_____

Australian Power Utilities

John Carter
Managing Director

Australian Power Utilities Inc
Block 7 Industrial Park
Canberra
Email: carter@apu.com

6 Complete the visitor form with information about yourself.

Language tip

Telling the time

Say *nine o'clock* or *nine am* for 9.00.
For 11.15 you can say *a quarter past /
after (US) eleven* or *eleven fifteen (am)*.
For 14.30 you can say *half past two* or *two
thirty (pm)*.
For 19.45 you can say *a quarter to eight* or
seven forty-five (pm).

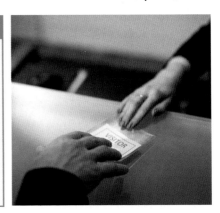

Speaking

7 You work at the reception of Lowis Engineering when a visitor arrives. Read
01–02 the instructions and welcome the visitor. Play Track 01 and speak after the
CD beep. You start. Then listen to Track 02 to compare your conversation.

You *Good morning madam, can I help you?*

Guest Yes, I have an appointment with Diane Kennedy for 11 o'clock.

You *(Ask her name.)*

Guest Jane Taylor from Taylor and Curtiss Consultants.

You *(Ask her to complete a security form.)*

Guest Can you give me a pen?

You *(Offer a pen.)*

Guest Thanks.

You *(Ask her to wear a visitor badge.)*

Guest Of course.

You *(Ask her to have a seat and say someone will come to get her.)*

Guest Good! Thanks for your help!

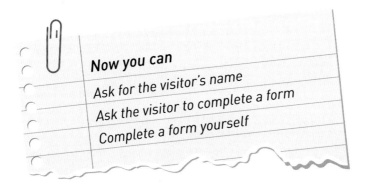

Now you can

Ask for the visitor's name

Ask the visitor to complete a form

Complete a form yourself

2   Company visitors

Welcoming visitors to a company | Introducing yourself | Taking visitors to a meeting

Conversation

DVD

1 Jasmine Goodman is Diane Kennedy's personal assistant at Lowis Engineering. She comes down to meet the visitors in reception. Read their conversation and watch the video. Who asked Jasmine to meet the guests?

Jasmine	**Excuse me, are you** John Carter and Paul Rogers?
John	Yes, we are. **I'm** John Carter and **this is** my colleague, Paul Rogers.
Jasmine	Hello, I'm Jasmine Goodman.
Paul	Hi.
John	Hi.
Jasmine	**Diane Kennedy asked me to meet you. Welcome to** Lowis Engineering.
Paul	Thank you.
John	Thank you.
Jasmine	**Come this way, please. We need to take the lift or, as you'd say, the elevator to the 3rd floor.**
Paul	It's a great building.
Jasmine	Yes, it is. It's a nice place to work.

Did you know?

In American English it is *elevator*. In British English it is *lift*. Also, the *first floor* in American English is the *ground floor* in British English.

Understanding

DVD

2 Watch again and answer the questions with *yes* and *no*.

1 Do John and Paul know Jasmine already?
2 Does Jasmine work at Lowis Engineering?
3 Do they need to take the lift?
4 Does Jasmine like where she works?

Key phrases

Meeting company guests

Excuse me, are you ... ?	*Come this way, please.*
I'm ... / this is	*We need to take the lift / elevator / stairs to the 3rd floor.*
Diane Kennedy asked me to meet you.	
Welcome to ... ,	

Practice

3 Join the two parts of the sentences together.

1 Excuse me,   A to our company.
2 I'm Paul and   B take the stairs to the 1st floor.
3 Ms Kennedy asked   C are you Paul Rogers?
4 Come this way,   D this is John.
5 Welcome   E me to meet you.
6 We need to   F please.

4 Put the words in the sentences into the correct order.

1 is my this John Carter I'm and colleague, Rogers Paul

_____.

2 floor We to take need the to lift the 3rd

_____.

3 Carter me, Excuse are Mr you

_____?

4 way, Come this please

_____.

5 Carter me asked Mr meet to you.

_____.

03 CD

5 Jasmine Goodman is meeting another visitor at reception. Complete the sentences. Then listen to Track 03 and check your answers.

Jasmine (1) _____ me, (2) _____ you Ms Ringwood?

Guest Yes, that's right.

Jasmine I'm Jasmine Goodman. Diane Kennedy (3) _____ me to meet you.

Guest Oh, hello Jasmine.

Jasmine (4) _____ to Lowis Engineering.

Guest Thank you!

Jasmine This way, please. We (5) _____ to take the lift to the 3rd floor.

Guest OK.

Language tip

Use *Excuse me* to start a conversation with someone you do not know or to interrupt someone when they are speaking.

Use ordinals – *first, second, third, fourth, fifth*, and so on – for floor numbers.

Speaking

6 Meet Mr Stenson at reception. Read the cues and welcome him. Play
Track 04 and speak after the beep. You start. Then listen to Track 05 to
compare your conversation.

04-05
CD

You	*Excuse me, are you Mr Stenson?*
Visitor	Yes, that's right.
You	*(Give your name and say your boss, Mr Brown, asked you to meet him – welcome him.)*
Visitor	Thank you very much.
You	*(Ask him to follow you to the lift – you need to go to the 8th floor.)*
Visitor	Of course. This is a great building.
You	*(Say it's a nice place to work.)*

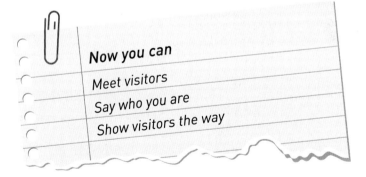

Now you can

Meet visitors

Say who you are

Show visitors the way

3   What do you do?

Talking about your work | Describing your job | Asking about somebody's job

Conversation

DVD

1   Jasmine Goodman is taking the visitors, John Carter and Paul Rogers, to the meeting room. They are waiting for the lift. Read their conversation and watch the video. What does Jasmine have to do in meetings?

John	So **what do you do**, Jasmine?
Jasmine	Oh, I'm Diane's personal assistant so **I answer the phone** and manage her schedule.
Paul	**Is she very busy** then?
Jasmine	Yes! She travels a lot. **I book all her plane tickets and hotels.**
John	I see. And **do you travel with her** sometimes?
Jasmine	No, not usually. I stay here and then **I'm responsible for** the office and **deal with** any problems.
Paul	You have a lot to do!
Jasmine	Yes. And in meetings, of course, **I take the minutes**.
Paul	... and **you look after visitors** to the company.
Jasmine	Yes, that's right! Ah, here it is. After you.
John	Thanks.

Did you know?

You can say **'sked**ule' or **'shed**ule' with the word *schedule*. In American English it is **'sked**ule' but with British English speakers you will hear both forms.

Understanding

DVD

2 Watch again. Are the sentences true (T) or false (F)?

1 Jasmine has lots of different responsibilities.   T / F
2 Jasmine usually travels with Diane.   T / F
3 Jasmine runs the meetings.   T / F
4 Jasmine helps the visitors.   T / F

Key phrases

Asking about and describing responsibilities

What do you do?	*I answer the phone.*
Is (s)he / Are you busy?	*I reply to emails.*
Do you travel with her?	*I'm responsible for … .*
I'm a personal assistant / salesman / receptionist.	*I deal with … .*
	I take the minutes at meetings.
I book all her plane tickets / hotels.	*I look after guests / visitors.*

Practice

3 Match the two halves to make word partners.

1	personal	A	with
2	responsible	B	to
3	take the	C	minutes
4	look	D	assistant
5	reply	E	for
6	deal	F	after

4 Match the two halves to make sentences.

1 I'm responsible   A after visitors to the company.

2 My colleague makes   B my work mobile after 6 o'clock.

3 The receptionist looks   C to my emails.

4 I always reply   D my flight reservations.

5 I don't answer   E for my boss's appointments.

5 Complete the sentences with information about your own work.

1 I'm a _____.

2 I'm responsible for _____.

3 I look after _____.

4 I reply to _____.

5 I deal with _____.

Language tip

When visitors ask you questions about your job, give as much information as you possibly can to keep the conversation going. Give full answers, for example, *Yes. And at meetings I take the minutes* **not** *Yes, I do.*

Speaking

6 A visitor asks you about your job. Play Track 06 and speak after the beep. Then listen to Track 07 to compare your conversation.

6–07 CD

Visitor	So, what do you do?
You	*(Answer the question.)*
Visitor	I see, that's interesting. Are you very busy?
You	*(Answer the question.)*
Visitor	And are you responsible for anything?
You	*(Answer the question.)*
Visitor	Do you do anything else?
You	*(Answer the question.)*

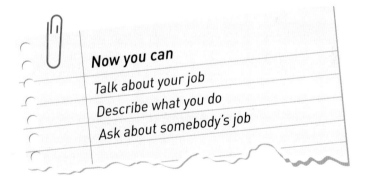

Now you can

Talk about your job

Describe what you do

Ask about somebody's job

4   Making visitors feel welcome

Looking after visitors | Offering visitors refreshments | Apologizing for a delay

Conversation

DVD

1   Jasmine takes John and Paul to the meeting room. Read their conversation and watch the video. Why does Jasmine call Paul 'Mr Rogers'?

Jasmine	Here we are. **Can I take your coat?**
John	Thank you.
Jasmine	**Would you like to sit down? I'm afraid Diane is still in a meeting. Would you like a cup of coffee?**
John	Er … .
Jasmine	Or a glass of water or juice?
John	I think I'd like some coffee, please.
Jasmine	**Would you like milk and sugar?**
John	Yes, please. Both. Thanks.
Jasmine	And **how about you**, Mr Rogers?
Paul	Please call me Paul. **I'd like some orange juice, please.**

Jasmine	**Here you are**, Paul.
Paul	Thanks very much.
Jasmine	**I'm sorry you have to wait, but Diane should be here soon.**
John	That's fine. Don't worry.

Did you know?

Another way to say *Don't worry* when someone apologizes is *No problem*. Australians also use the phrase *No worries*.

In American English people often ask if you want cream in your coffee, not milk.

Understanding

DVD

2 Watch the video again. Are the sentences true (T) or false (F)?

1 Diane Kennedy is waiting for John and Paul in the meeting room.   T / F
2 Jasmine offers John and Paul something to drink.   T / F
3 Paul wants some coffee.   T / F
4 Jasmine is sorry because Diane is late.   T / F
5 John and Paul are angry that Diane Kennedy is late.   T / F

Key phrases

Polite offers and apologies

Can I take your coat(s)?	*How / What about you, … ?*
Would you like to sit down / have a seat?	*I'd like some orange juice, please.*
I'm afraid that … is (still) in a meeting.	*Here you are.*
Would you like some / a cup of coffee?	*I'm sorry you have to wait, but … should be here soon.*
Would you like milk and sugar?	

Practice

3 Put the words in the sentences into the correct order.

1 tea you Would a like cup of

_____?

2 please like some I'd coffee,

_____.

3 you down like to Would sit

_____?

4 sorry to you I'm wait have

_____.

5 Carter here soon should Mr be

_____.

6 you sugar like milk Would and

_____?

7 afraid Mrs White I'm meeting is still in a

_____.

8 are you Here

_____.

4 Match the sentences.

1 Would you like to sit down?   A Just milk, please.
2 Would you like a cup of coffee?   B Thank you.
3 I'm sorry you have to wait.   C Please call me Paul.
4 Would you like milk and sugar?   D Don't worry.
5 What about you, Mr Rogers?   E No, but I'd like some water.

5 Complete the sentences with words from the box.

like	afraid	soon	have	here
please	should	in	take	some

1 I'm _____ Mr Carter is _____ a meeting.
2 Would you _____ to _____ a seat?
3 _____ you are.
4 Can I _____ your coat?
5 I'd like _____ coffee, _____.
6 Ms Goodman _____ be here _____.

Language tip

When you offer a visitor refreshments, make sure you sound friendly and enthusiastic. You can do this by making your voice go up at the end of the question, for example, *Would you like a cup of coffee?* ↗

Speaking

6 You have two visitors to your office. Read the instructions and look after
08-09 them until your boss arrives. Play Track 08 and speak after the beep. You
CD start. Then listen to Track 09 to compare your conversation.

You	*(Ask if you can take the visitors' coats.)*
Visitor 1	Thank you.
Visitor 2	Here you are.
You	*(Offer them a seat.)*
Visitor 1	Thanks.
You	*(Ask if they want some coffee or juice.)*
Visitor 1	I'd like some coffee, please.
You	*(Ask what Visitor 2 – Mr Carter – would like.)*
Visitor 2	I'd like some orange juice.
You	*(Say your boss, Ms Kennedy, is in a meeting.)*
Visitor 1	No problem.
You	*(Say she will arrive soon.)*
Visitor 2	Thanks.

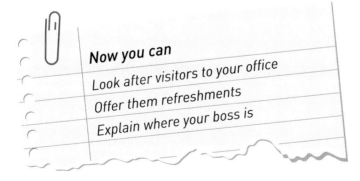

Now you can

Look after visitors to your office

Offer them refreshments

Explain where your boss is

5   Small talk

Making conversation | Checking things are OK | Finding out what people like

Conversation

DVD

1   Jasmine is talking to John and Paul while they wait for Diane Kennedy, her boss. Read their conversation and watch the video. Does Diane arrive for the meeting?

Jasmine	So, **how was your flight?**
John	Oh, it was fine. But we had to check in very early this morning at Frankfurt airport.
Jasmine	Oh yes, airport security takes such a long time these days. **How's the hotel?**
Paul	Very nice. Thank you for making the reservation for us.
Jasmine	My pleasure. **Is this your first time here?**
John	Well, not to London, of course. But it's our first time to your company.
Paul	Yes. And we're very interested in your products.
Jasmine	Good. **How long are you staying in** London?
Paul	A week. **What should we do** at the weekend?

Jasmine	Mmm ... **do you like** football? You know, soccer?
John	Yes, very much.
Jasmine	**Would you like to** see a Chelsea match this weekend? I could get you some tickets.
Paul	Thank you, that's a great idea!
John	Fantastic!
Jasmine	You're welcome. By the way, I've made reservation for lunch for you and Diane at a French restaurant near here. Is that OK?
John	Excellent! Thank you.
Paul	That sounds great.
Jasmine	Good. Well, **I'll find out where Diane is and let her know you're here**.
Paul	Fine.

Did you know?

Soccer in American English is called *football* in British English. *Football* in American English refers to *American football*.

Understanding

DVD

2 **Watch again and answer the questions.**

1 Where did John and Paul fly from?
2 Who made the hotel reservation for John and Paul?
3 Have they been to Lowis Engineering before?
4 What does Jasmine offer to organize for the weekend?
5 Where will they have lunch today?

Key phrases

Making small talk

How was your flight / trip / journey?	*Do you like ... ?*
How's / How is the hotel?	*Would you like to ... ?*
Is this your first time here?	*I'll find out where ... is and tell her / him you're here.*
How long are you staying in ... ?	
What should we do ... ?	

3 Join the two parts of the sentences together.

1	How was	**A** where Mr Brown is.
2	How is	**B** time in Paris?
3	Is this your first	**C** the hotel?
4	How long are	**D** your flight?
5	Do you	**E** do in the evening?
6	What should we	**F** you staying in Berlin?
7	I'll check	**G** like Italian food?

4 Write the questions to go with the answers.

1	_____	No, I often come here.
2	_____	It's very comfortable. And close to the centre!
3	_____	Terrible. The weather was bad.
4	_____	Theatre? Yes, I do. Very much.
5	_____	'The Lion King'? Yes, I would.
6	_____	Only three days, unfortunately.

Language tip

Use *Do you like … ?* when you want to know somebody's opinion, for example, *Do you like football?*

Use *Would you like … ?* to make an offer, for example, *Would you like a cup of coffee?*

Use *By the way* when you want to change the topic of conversation.

When someone says *Thank you*, reply with *My pleasure* or *You're welcome*.

Speaking

5 Make small talk with a visitor from London. Read the instructions and talk to your visitor while you are waiting for your boss to arrive. Play Track 10 and speak after the beep. You start. Then listen to Track 11 to compare your conversation.

10–11
CD

You	*(Ask about the flight from London.)*
Visitor	Oh, not very good. The weather in London is terrible at the moment. It's nice to see some sunshine here.
You	*(Agree. Ask about her hotel.)*
Visitor	It's very nice. Thank you for organizing it.
You	*(Reply then ask if she has visited your town before)*
Visitor	Yes, this is my first time. What should I do in the evening?
You	*(Ask if she likes your country's food.)*
Visitor	Very much!
You	*(Ask if she wants to try a local restaurant this evening.)*
Visitor	Oh, yes! Very much. Thank you.
You	*(Reply. Then ask how long she is staying in your town.)*
Visitor	Until Friday. Then I fly back to London.
You	*(Offer to go to find your boss.)*
Visitor	Thanks a lot.

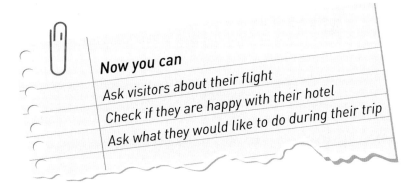

Now you can

Ask visitors about their flight

Check if they are happy with their hotel

Ask what they would like to do during their trip

6   Introductions

Making introductions | Meeting people | Using first or given names

Conversation

DVD

1   Jasmine finds her boss, Diane Kennedy, and brings her to meet two visitors. Read their conversation and watch the video. Why doesn't Diane introduce Jasmine to Paul and John?

Jasmine	Here she is! Diane, **I'd like to introduce** John Carter and Paul Rogers from Australian Power Utilities.
Diane	**Nice to meet you!**
John	**Nice to meet you too**, Ms Kennedy. I'm John Carter.
Diane	**Please, call me** Diane!
John	**Fine, Diane. And I'm John. This is my colleague** Paul Rogers.
Paul	**Pleased to meet you**, Diane.
Diane	**Pleased to meet you too**, Paul. And **I see you've met my assistant Jasmine already**. I'm very sorry I'm late. I'm afraid my last meeting went on for a while.
John	Oh, don't worry. Jasmine took care of us.
Diane	Good. So, please have a seat.
Paul	Thanks.

Did you know?

Sometimes people say *How do you do?* when you meet them for the first time but it is a bit formal. The correct reply is also *How do you do?* It is not a real question.

Understanding

DVD

2   Watch again. Are the sentences true (T) or false (F)?

1   John and Paul have met Diane before.   T / F

2   Diane is very apologetic about being late.   T / F

3   Diane was in a long meeting.   T / F

4   Diane asks John to use her first name.   T / F

Key phrases

Introductions

I'd like to introduce ... from ...?	*This is my colleague ... .*
Nice to meet you.	*Pleased to meet you.*
Nice to meet you too.	*Pleased to meet you too.*
Please, call me ...	*I see you've met ... already.*
Fine. And I'm ...	

Practice

3   Put the words in the sentences into the correct order.

1   to John meet Nice you,

   _____.

2   is Diane colleague, This Kennedy my

   _____.

3   meet to you Nice too

   _____.

4   Carter see you've already my manager I John met

   _____.

5   Ms to meet you, Pleased Goodman

   _____.

6   Jasmine me call Please

   _____.

4 Complete the sentences.

1 Fine. And _____ Paul.
2 I see you've met Diane _____ .
3 This _____ my _____ John.
4 Nice to meet you _____ .
5 I'd _____ to _____ Paul Rogers from APU.
6 Please _____ me Paul.

5 Put the sentences into the correct order to make a conversation. Then listen to Track 12 to check your answers.

	Mr Kline	OK, but it was a bit late taking off.
	Diane	Nice to meet you, Mr Kline.
	Mr Kline	Nice to meet you too. But please call me Mike.
1	Jasmine	Diane, can I introduce you to Mr Kline?
	Mr Kline	Thank you.
	Mr Kline	No, thanks.
	Diane	So how was your flight?
	Diane	And would you like some coffee?
	Diane	Of course. And I'm Diane. Would you like to take a seat?

Language tip

Always check that visitors have been introduced to everybody in the room. Notice how Diane does this with *And I see you've met my assistant Jasmine already.*

Speaking

6 You are meeting a visitor to your company. Your colleague introduces you. Play Track 13 and speak after the beep. Then listen to Track 14 to compare your conversation.

13–14
CD

Colleague	So here we are! I'd like to introduce Lee Toms from DPU.
You	*(Greet Mr Toms.)*
Lee	Nice to meet you too but please call me Lee.
You	*(Tell him your first name and ask him to take a seat.)*
Lee	Thank you.
You	*(Apologize for being late.)*
Lee	No problem.
You	*(Offer coffee.)*
Lee	No, thanks.
You	*(Ask about Lee's journey.)*
Lee	It was fine. No problem.

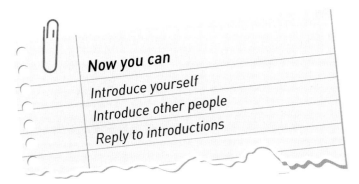

Now you can

Introduce yourself

Introduce other people

Reply to introductions

7　An inquiry by email

Writing a formal email | Explaining what you need | Asking for information

Email

1　Jasmine Goodman from Lowis Engineering is organizing a conference. Who is she writing to?

From:　　jasmine.goodman@lowis.com
To:　　　info@anchorhotels.co.uk
Date:　　February 7
Subject:　Event for Lowis Engineering

Dear Sir or Madam

I am writing to ask about conference facilities at your London hotel.

On May 3, Lowis Engineering is organizing an event for 500 major customers. **We would like to** demonstrate some of our equipment and present information about our products to our guests. **Please let me know if** your conference facilities are available on this date.

I would be grateful if you could send me information about the presentation equipment, room sizes and catering facilities in your hotel. **Please include** a telephone number and a contact person I can call to discuss details.

I look forward to hearing from you.

Yours faithfully

Jasmine Goodman

Lowis Engineering

Did you know?

In American English, when you do not know the name of the person you are writing to, you begin an email like this *To Whom It May Concern* and finish *Best regards*. In British English you begin *Dear Sir or Madam* and end *Yours faithfully*, as above.

Understanding

2 Read the email again and choose the best answer A, B or C for each question.

1 Lowis Engineering is organizing a conference for:
   A tourists in London
   B company staff
   C people it does business with

2 May 3 is the date when:
   A Jasmine is writing the email
   B the conference will take place
   C the hotel says the conference can take place

3 Jasmine wants:
   A the name of somebody at the hotel
   B to visit the hotel
   C to check the costs

Key phrases

Asking for information

I am writing to ask about … .	*I would be grateful if you could … .*
We would like to … .	*Please include … .*
Please let me know if … .	*I look forward to hearing from you.*

Practice

3 Join the two parts of the sentences together.

1 Please let me know
2 I would be grateful if
3 I am writing
4 I look forward to
5 We would
6 Please include

A to ask you about your prices.
B like to organize an event.
C if you can meet me.
D a photograph of the facilities.
E meeting you soon.
F you could organize a meeting.

4 Put the words in the sentences into the correct order.

1 your include address Please number telephone and

_____ .

2 like would to We to invite you presentation a

_____ .

3 I be grateful could you if send brochure us would a

_____ .

4 let me is know for this time you possible Please if

_____ .

5 I forward look to Tuesday seeing on you

_____ .

5 Read this email from Jasmine to an event management company. Find and correct the mistake in each numbered line.

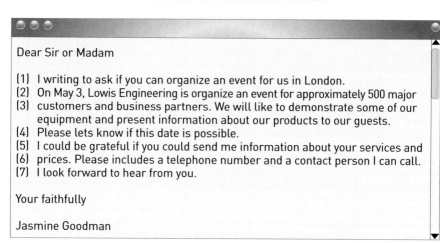

Dear Sir or Madam

(1) I writing to ask if you can organize an event for us in London.
(2) On May 3, Lowis Engineering is organize an event for approximately 500 major
(3) customers and business partners. We will like to demonstrate some of our
equipment and present information about our products to our guests.
(4) Please lets know if this date is possible.
(5) I could be grateful if you could send me information about your services and
(6) prices. Please includes a telephone number and a contact person I can call.
(7) I look forward to hear from you.

Your faithfully

Jasmine Goodman

Language tip

Use the present continuous tense to talk about what you are doing now, for example, *I am writing to ask about ...* and to talk about future plans, for example, *On May 3, Lowis Engineering is organizing ...* .

In formal emails use the uncontracted forms, for example, *I am writing ...* not *I'm writing ...* or *I would be grateful ...* not *I'd be grateful ...* .

See page 149 for more information on the present continuous.

Writing

6 Your boss, Joanna Timms, wants you to write an email. Use your notes to help you. You work for Crayton Car Rentals.

> Write to the Event Manager, Carlton Hotel.
> We need a large room for our Annual General Meeting in New York:
> Date: April 19
> Numbers: 300 guests
> We need information about:
> 1) Room size
> 2) Presentation equipment
> 3) Catering
> 4) Costs

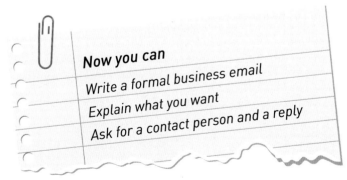

Now you can
Write a formal business email
Explain what you want
Ask for a contact person and a reply

8   A reply to an inquiry

Sending information | Describing special offers | Providing contact details

Email

1   Jon Martin from Anchor Hotels writes an email to Jasmine Goodman to tell
her about their conference facilities. What special offer does he mention?

From: j.martin@anchorhotels.co.uk
To: jasmine.goodman@lowis.com
Date: February 8
Subject: Re: Event for Lowis Engineering

Dear Ms Goodman

Thank you for your email of February 7. **With reference to your** request for
conference facility information, **please find attached** a PDF file with a
description of our London hotel. The information can also be seen online at
www.Anchorhotels.com.

I am pleased to inform you that we are offering a discount of 25% for any
reservation made before the end of February. We still have rooms available for
the date of your conference, May 3.

If you would like further information about our services, **please contact me on**
020 8307 4001.

Yours sincerely

Jon Martin
Conference Manager – Anchor Hotels

Did you know?

In American English when you write 01/03/2012 you mean January 3, 2012.
In British English when you write 01/03/2012 you mean March 1, 2012.
To make sure there is no misunderstanding, spell it out, for example, February 7, 2014.

Understanding

2 Read the email again. Are the sentences true (T) or false (F)?

1 Lowis Engineering is organizing a conference for February 7. T / F
2 The hotel information can only be found on the website. T / F
3 If Jasmine makes a reservation before March 1, she can get a discount. T / F
4 The hotel is fully booked on May 3. T / F
5 Jon Martin is the conference manager at Anchor Hotels. T / F

Key phrases

Giving information

Thank you for your email of … .	*We are offering a discount of X%.*
With reference to your .. .	*If you would like further information*
Please find attached / enclosed … .	*about … .*
I am pleased to inform you that … .	*Please contact me on … .*

Practice

3 Complete the sentences with words from the box.

available	conference facilities	contact
discount	price information	email

1 Our company is offering a _____ of 10%.
2 Thank you for your _____ of October 19.
3 Please find enclosed _____ for our conference rooms.
4 With reference to your request for _____ information, please find attached a brochure as a PDF file.
5 Please _____ me on 0207 98 5151.
6 I am pleased to inform you that we have a meeting room _____ on March 27.

4 Put the words in the sentences into the correct order.

1 you 0207 98 5151 like further on would information, If contact me

_____.

2 the am inform pleased to you that this date is available I

_____.

3 morning Thank your for you phone call this

_____.

4 find service our information Please attached

_____.

5 reference of to 27 your With email March

_____.

5 Put the sentences in this email to Jasmine Goodman from another hotel in the correct order.

Dear Ms Goodman

Please find enclosed information about our conference equipment and prices. [ ]
With reference to the date of your event, we have rooms available at that time. [ ]
Yours sincerely [ ]
If you would like further information, please let me know. [ ]
Thank you for your phone call to my assistant this afternoon. [1]
We are pleased to inform you that we have a special offer for catering facilities in May. [ ]

Yours sincerely

Priti Makesch

Language tip

If you have a lot of similar emails to write, use one that has several key phrases as a model which you can change slightly according to each different situation.

Writing

6 You work in a hotel. Listen to Track 15 to hear this voicemail from your boss, Fran Stein, and then complete the email to the customer.

15
CD

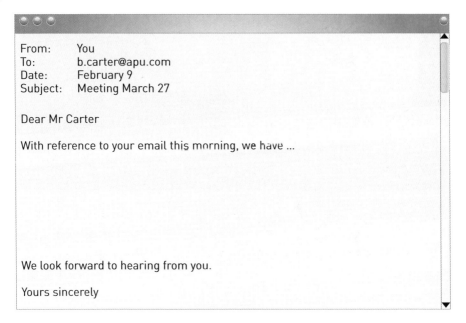

From: You
To: b.carter@apu.com
Date: February 9
Subject: Meeting March 27

Dear Mr Carter

With reference to your email this morning, we have ...

We look forward to hearing from you.

Yours sincerely

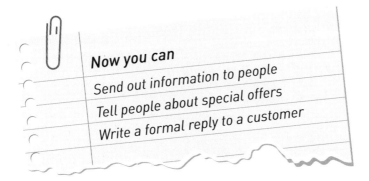

Now you can
Send out information to people
Tell people about special offers
Write a formal reply to a customer

9   A follow-up email

Writing an informal email | Making a request | Asking for help

Email

1 Jasmine Goodman writes to Jon Martin about the Lowis event. How many things does she want Jon to do?

From: jasmine.goodman@lowis.com
To: j.martin@anchorhotels.co.uk
Date: March 20
Subject: Lowis event on May 3

Dear Jon

Can you help me? Would you mind arranging a visit for my manager, Diane Kennedy, to see your conference facilities at the hotel? She wants to see what they are like. **Would you be able to** arrange this for next week?

Secondly, **could you** arrange a gift for each guest at the event? **Are you able to** do this for less than €50 per guest?

If that is OK, then could you send a new offer with the total price?

Many thanks for your help.

Best wishes

Jasmine

PS I can't open the pictures of the conference rooms you sent. **Please advise.**

Did you know?

You can use *Best wishes* or *Best regards* at the end of an email either to somebody you know well or don't know at all.

Understanding

2 Read the email again and choose the best answer A, B or C for each question.

1 This email is informal because:

A it's short

B Jasmine uses Mr Martin's first name

C Jasmine uses a PS at the end

2 Diane Kennedy wants to:

A test the conference facilities

B go to the Anchor Hotel

C cancel the event

3 Jasmine wants Jon:

A to buy her a gift

B to buy one gift for all the guests

C to buy one gift for each guest

4 The present should cost:

A under €50

B over €50

C €50

5 Jasmine is having problems:

A with a document Jon sent

B with some photos Jon sent

C with some video Jon sent

Key phrases

Asking for help

Can you help me?	*Could you ...?*
Would you mind +ing ...?	*Are you able to ...?*
Would you be able to ...?	*Please advise.*

Practice

3 Join the two parts of the requests for help together.

1	Are you able to	A	reply to this email?
2	Can you help me	B	me as soon as possible?
3	Would you mind	C	able to meet me?
4	Could you contact	D	helping me?
5	Would you be	E	send a new offer?

4 Put the words in the requests into the correct order.

1 the tomorrow you to Are come to able meeting

_____?

2 you sending possible mind a new contract as Would as soon

_____?

3 you to translation send the Paul Could Rogers

_____?

4 be you able Would to me help

_____?

5 you by Friday finish the Can report

_____?

5 Make a list of three to five tasks you have to do this week at work.

1 _____

2 _____

3 _____

4 _____

5 _____

You are going on vacation tomorrow, but your tasks aren't finished yet. Ask a colleague for help.

Could you _write the meeting report?_

Are you able to _____?

Would you mind _____?

Would you be able to _____?

Language tip

Use *Would you mind +ing …?* when you want to ask somebody to do something difficult. Note it is always followed by the *+ing* form, for example, *Would you mind organizing / calling / visiting / presenting … .*

To say *yes* to a request with *Would you mind … ?* use *No, not at all* or *Of course not.*

Writing

6 Jon Martin wants his assistant, Katy Jones, to show Diane Kennedy around the Anchor Hotel. Complete the email he wrote to her.

From: j.martin@anchorhotels.co.uk
To: k.jones@anchorhotels.co.uk
Date: March 28
Subject: Visit from important customer tomorrow

Dear Katy

Tomorrow, Diane Kennedy from Lowis Engineering is coming but I'm not well so can you (1) _____ me? She is arranging an event on May 3 so could you (2) _____ her the conference facilities?

Also, are you (3) _____ to take her to lunch? I want her to see how good the catering is.

Finally, would you (4) _____ showing her the gifts we plan for the guests at the event? Her assistant, Jasmine Goodman, ordered them.

Is this OK with you? Please (5) _____ if there is any problem.

Best wishes

Jon

Now you can
Write an informal business email
Explain what you need
Ask for help with something

10 A reply to a follow-up email

Writing an informal reply | Making suggestions | Offering help

Email

1 Jon Martin, the conference manager from Anchor Hotels, writes to Jasmine Goodman at Lowis Engineering with some suggestions. How many suggestions does he make?

From: j.martin@anchorhotels.co.uk
To: jasmine.goodman@lowis.com
Date: March 21
Subject: Lowis event on May 3

Dear Jasmine

Thanks for your email and your requests. I have put my answer after your questions:

1) *Would you mind arranging a visit for my manager, Diane Kennedy?*
Not at all. **If you like, we could** give Ms Kennedy a tour of the facilities and offer her lunch.

2) Could you arrange a gift for each guest at the event?
Yes, no problem. **What about including** a personal card from you or Ms Kennedy with the gift?
3) Are you able to do this for less than €50 per guest?
Of course. **Why don't you look** at the attached list of possible gifts and tell me what you think is best?
4) Could you send a new offer with the total price?
Yes. I haven't finished the new offer yet, but I will do it tomorrow. **Would you like me to** send it to Ms Kennedy as well?
5) I can't open the pictures of the conference rooms you sent.
Have you tried opening the pictures in Microsoft PowerPoint? Or **should I** send you the photos in the post?

I hope these suggestions help. **Let me know if you need anything else.**

Best regards

Jon

Did you know?

You can respond to email requests by using the original email and adding comments or replies below in a different colour or preceded by your initials.

Understanding

2 Read the email again and answer the questions.

1 When Diane visits the Anchor Hotel in central London, what will Jon offer her?
2 What does Jon suggest including with the guests' gifts?
3 Why does Jasmine ask for a new offer?
4 What does Jon offer to send Jasmine in the post?

Key phrases

Making suggestions	Offering help
What / How about +ing ... ?	*If you like, we could ... .*
Why don't you ...?	*Would you like me to ...?*
Have you tried +ing ... ?	*Should I ...?*
	Let me know if you need anything else.

Practice

3 Put the words in the sentences into the correct order.

1 don't you a meeting Why arrange

_____?

2 you like me to send an Would email

_____?

3 you offices moving Have tried

_____?

4 What meeting of about the time the changing

_____?

5 me Let know if date you another need

_____.

6 I appointment change the Should

_____?

4 A colleague at work tells you he can't finish a report because he has too much work. Offer him some suggestions and complete the sentences with your own information.

1 What about _____?

2 How about _____?

3 If you like, I could _____ .

4 Let me know if you need _____ .

5 Why don't you _____?

5 Read this email from Jon's assistant, Katy Jones. Find and correct the mistake in each numbered line.

Dear Jon

(1) Here are few suggestions for the Lowis Web event we're organizing in May in the central London hotel.

(2) Who don't we use the conference rooms next to the bistro on the top floor?

(3) The view of London is great. And how about have a celebrity chef for the catering?

(4) My sister works with a celebrity chef and, if you like, he could ask how much it costs to hire him for the day.

(5) Also, have you thought about organize some music? It would be nice for the breaks, I think.

(6) Would you like me check the prices for a band?

(7) Let me know if you needs anything else.

Regards

Katy

Language tip

Use the present perfect tense – *I have put my answers after your questions* – to talk about something done in the past that is still relevant now. We never use it with a fixed time expression, for example, *yesterday / last year*.

See page 153 for more information about the present perfect tense.

Writing

6 A colleague of yours has to organize an office party. Send her an email with some suggestions. Use the notes to help you.

> Place – use company cafeteria, comfortable
> Time – start 6 pm, finish midnight – need to work next day!
> Music – live band. Offer to contact friend in band 'The Big Noise'?
> Anything else?

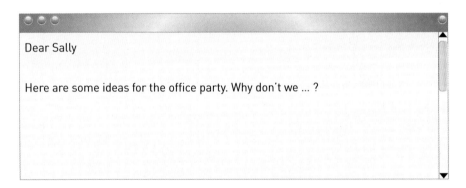

Dear Sally

Here are some ideas for the office party. Why don't we ... ?

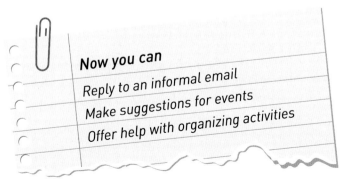

Now you can

Reply to an informal email

Make suggestions for events

Offer help with organizing activities

11 Invitations

Writing invitations | Describing events | Giving information about events

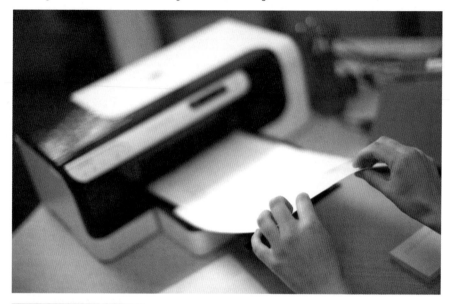

Emails

1 Jasmine Goodman is inviting different people to the Lowis event that she is organizing. What is the difference between the two emails?

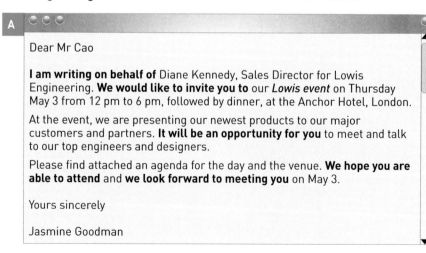

A

Dear Mr Cao

I am writing on behalf of Diane Kennedy, Sales Director for Lowis Engineering. **We would like to invite you to** our *Lowis event* on Thursday May 3 from 12 pm to 6 pm, followed by dinner, at the Anchor Hotel, London.

At the event, we are presenting our newest products to our major customers and partners. **It will be an opportunity for you** to meet and talk to our top engineers and designers.

Please find attached an agenda for the day and the venue. **We hope you are able to attend** and **we look forward to meeting you** on May 3.

Yours sincerely

Jasmine Goodman

B

Dear John

Diane **asked me to write to you**. On May 3 we are organizing a *Lowis event* for our major customers and partners to present our latest products at the Anchor Hotel, London. It starts at noon and there will be a dinner in the evening. **Are you free on this date**, and **would you and Paul like to come**?

The agenda for the day and the location details are attached. **I hope to see you on** May 3.

Best wishes

Jasmine

Did you know?

Another way to say *noon* in British English is *midday*.

Understanding

2   Read the emails again. Are the sentences true (T) or false (F)?

1 Jasmine is writing for Diane.	T / F
2 The event is for the whole day.	T / F
3 After the event, the visitors can do something together.	T / F
4 In the second email, Jasmine only invites John.	T / F

Key phrases

Invitations

I am writing on behalf of … . (formal)	*X asked me to write to you. (informal)*
We would like to invite you to … . (formal)	*Are you free on this date / at this time / in June? (informal)*
It will be an opportunity for you … . (formal)	
We hope you are able to attend … . (formal)	*Would you like to come? (informal)*
We look forward to meeting you / seeing you there. (formal)	*I hope to see you on … . (informal)*

3 Put the words in the sentences into the correct order.

1 Chairman It will an to our opportunity be for you meet

_____.

2 Thursday like to would invite you meeting to a on We

_____.

3 lunch you like Would to to come

_____?

4 hope able you We are to conference attend the

_____.

5 Are o'clock free at 6 meeting you for a

_____?

4 You are writing an email to a colleague of yours to invite him to dinner at the weekend. Some of the phrases in the email are too formal. Change the numbered phrases to something more informal. Remember that in some cases, a question can be used to make a suggestion.

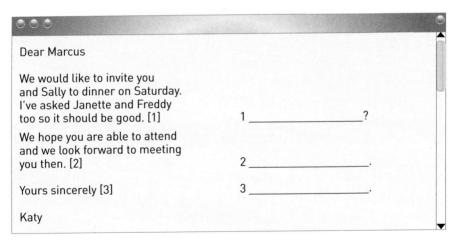

Dear Marcus

We would like to invite you
and Sally to dinner on Saturday.
I've asked Janette and Freddy
too so it should be good. [1]   1 _____?

We hope you are able to attend
and we look forward to meeting
you then. [2]   2 _____.

Yours sincerely [3]   3 _____.

Katy

Language tip

Use *in* with months and seasons, for example, *in January, in the summer.*
Use *on* with days of the week, for example, *on Saturday.*
Use *at* with exact times, for example, *at six o'clock.*
Use *at* with public holidays, for example, *at Christmas(time).*
In British English, use *at the weekend*, and in American English *on the weekend.*

Writing

5   Your boss, Joanna Timms, wants you to invite a very important customer to a meeting and then lunch. Use your boss's notes to write the invitation.

Please write to Helmut Probst, Order Manager at Tycoil Electronics. Invite him to our key customer meeting Thursday morning, April 7. I want him to meet our Managing Director, Tim King, and the sales team.
Then I will take him to lunch at the Ritz.
Thanks!

Joanna – Sales Director, CMCX Ltd

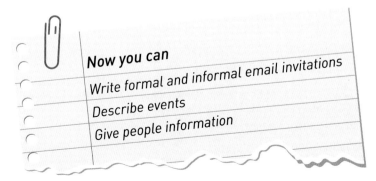

Now you can

Write formal and informal email invitations

Describe events

Give people information

12 Replies to invitations

Accepting an invitation | Saying no to an invitation | Giving reasons

Emails

1 Look at these three replies to Jasmine Goodman's invitations to the Lowis Engineering event. Who accepts the invitation and who doesn't?

A

Dear Ms Goodman

Thank you for your invitation to my manager, Mr Cao, for the event at Lowis Engineering on May 3. Mr Cao **is pleased to accept your invitation** and will attend from 12.00 until 18.00 and the dinner event at the Anchor Hotel.

Yours sincerely

Jenny Chang

B

Dear Ms Goodman

With reference to your email of March 7, **unfortunately Ms Schmidt is unable to attend** the Lowis Engineering event on May 3 **due to** a business trip on that date. **We wish you success with your event.**

Best regards

Eva Fleck

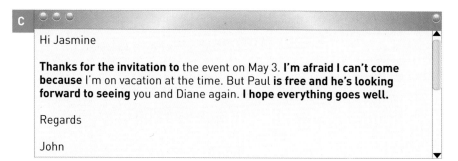

C

Hi Jasmine

Thanks for the invitation to the event on May 3. **I'm afraid I can't come because** I'm on vacation at the time. But Paul **is free and he's looking forward to seeing** you and Diane again. **I hope everything goes well.**

Regards

John

Understanding

2 Read the emails again. Find somebody who:

1 is on holiday on May 3.

2 will come to all of the Lowis event.

3 is on a business trip.

4 is looking forward to seeing Jasmine and Diane.

Key phrases

Accepting or declining an invitation

Thank you for your invitation to	*Unfortunately, XYZ is unable to attend ... due to ... .*
Thanks for the invitation to	
XYZ is pleased to accept your invitation.	*I'm afraid I can't come because ... .*
XYZ is free and is looking forward to seeing	*We wish you success with your event.*
	I hope everything goes well.

Practice

3 Look again at the phrases in the Key phrases box. Write F (formal) or I (informal) against each phrase.

4 Complete the sentences with information from the box.

attend	due	free	because of	pleased	success

1 Mr Carter is unable to _____ the conference.

2 I wish you _____ with your workshop.

3 Ms Kennedy is _____ to accept your invitation.

4 This is _____ to another appointment.

5 I'm _____ on May 3 and I'm looking forward to being there.

6 I can't be there _____ a business trip.

5 Put the words in the sentences into the correct order.

1 you for on invitation Thank the the to Friday meeting

_____ .

2 hope goes everything We on Friday well

_____ .

3 to Goodman a business Ms Due is attend unable trip to due

_____ .

4 Mr invitation Rogers your pleased to is accept

_____ .

6 A colleague has been invited to a sales conference by a supplier to see their latest products. She has written an email but she wants you to check it. The highlighted parts are too informal. Rewrite the highlighted parts more formally.

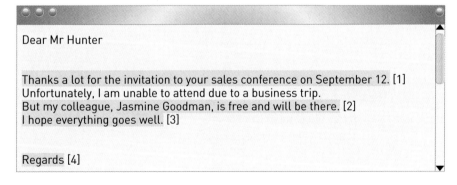

Dear Mr Hunter

Thanks a lot for the invitation to your sales conference on September 12. [1]
Unfortunately, I am unable to attend due to a business trip.
But my colleague, Jasmine Goodman, is free and will be there. [2]
I hope everything goes well. [3]

Regards [4]

1

2

3

4

Language tip

If you cannot accept an invitation, always give a reason why, for example, *due to a business trip* or *because I'm on holiday (UK) / vacation (US)*. Use something like *unfortunately* or *I'm afraid* to make your reason sound more polite.

Writing

7 You have an invitation to an anniversary. Write an answer either accepting the invitation or explaining why you can't go.

Dear Mr Rogers

We would like to invite you to our company's **25th Anniversary** on Thursday July 6 from 6 o'clock until midnight, followed by fireworks.

Please find attached information about the day. We hope you are able to attend and we look forward to seeing you on July 4.

Yours sincerely

Katy Jones

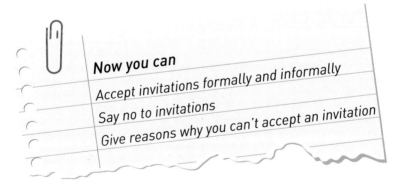

Now you can

Accept invitations formally and informally

Say no to invitations

Give reasons why you can't accept an invitation

13 Incoming calls

Answering the phone | Explaining somebody is not available | Calling back

Telephone calls

1 Listen to the two telephone conversations. Which department does Alan want? Why can't Diane answer the phone?

16 CD

A

Sally	Lowis Engineering, Sally Tyrone speaking. Can I help you?
Alan	Hello, this is Alan Jay from Texas Consultants. I'd like to speak to somebody in your Sales Department, please.
Sally	**Please hold. I'll put you through to** Ms Kennedy. ... Hello, Mr Jay? **I'm sorry but her line's busy at the moment. Can you hold?**
Alan	Er, yes, OK.
Sally	**I'm afraid she's still engaged. Can you call back later?**
Alan	Hm. All right. Goodbye.
Sally	Goodbye.

B

Jasmine	Diane Kennedy's phone, Jasmine Goodman speaking.
John	Hello, Jasmine. John Carter from APU here. Is Diane there?
Jasmine	Oh hi, John. **I'm afraid she's not available at the moment.** She's in a meeting.

John	Oh, I see. I need to speak to her today.
Jasmine	Well, the meeting is until 11 o'clock. Can you call back later?
John	Yes, OK. **I'll call back at** 11.30. Is that OK?
Jasmine	Yes, that's fine.
John	Good. Thanks, Jasmine. Bye.
Jasmine	Bye, bye John. **Maybe speak to you later.**

Did you know?

In some companies, you can dial somebody's number directly. In other companies, you need to speak to a receptionist or operator first.

Understanding

2 Listen again and choose the best answer A, B or C for each question.

16
CD

1 Alan can't speak to Diane because:
   A she isn't there
   B she doesn't want to speak to him
   C she's talking to somebody else on the phone

2 Sally asks Alan:
   A to hold on to the phone
   B to wait for a moment
   C to put the phone down

3 John wants to:
   A visit Diane today
   B speak to Diane today
   C have a meeting with Diane

4 John says:
   A he will call back
   B send an email
   C wait for a call from Diane

Key phrases

Dealing with calls

Please hold.	*Can you call back later?*
I'll put you through to … .	*I'm afraid she's not available at the moment.*
I'm sorry but her line's busy at the moment.	
Can you hold?	*I'll call back at … .*
I'm afraid she's still engaged (UK) / on the line (US).	*(Maybe) speak to you later.*

Practice

3 Join the two parts of the sentences together.

1	I'll put you through	A	you later.
2	Can you	B	available at the moment.
3	I'll call back	C	to Jasmine Goodman.
4	I'm afraid she's not	D	still on the line.
5	I'm afraid she's	E	hold?
6	Speak to	F	hold.
7	Please	G	this afternoon.

4 Put the words in the sentences into the correct order.

1 sorry moment busy but Mr at I'm Carter's line is the

_____ .

2 boss later will My call back

_____ .

3 afraid on a he's business I'm trip

_____ .

4 you back morning call Can tomorrow

_____ ?

5 put through the you to Sales I'll Department

_____ .

5 Write a sentence on the left to go with the response on the right.

1 _____   OK. I'll call back after lunch then.

2 _____   She's in a meeting? How long for?

3 _____   The Sales Department? Yes, thank you.

4 _____   No, I can't hold. I'll call back later.

5 _____   Still engaged? OK, I'll hold.

Language tip

Use *will* to show that you have decided to do something, for example,
The phone's ringing! – Don't worry, I'll answer it!

I'll call back at 11.00.

See page 152 for more information.

Language tip

If you have to say a colleague isn't available to speak on the phone, it's polite to apologize and explain what they are doing, for example, *I'm afraid he's in a meeting / on a business trip.*

Speaking

7–18
CD

6 A customer calls your company to speak to a colleague. Play Track 17 and speak after the beep. Then listen to Track 18 to compare your conversation.

Customer	Can I speak to Mr Rogers, please?
You	*(Tell him Mr Rogers is in a meeting.)*
Customer	Oh, I see. Well, can I speak to Pauline Coates in the Sales Department?
You	*(Tell him you will put him through.)*
Customer	Thanks.
You	*(Apologize and tell him that Ms Coates' line is busy.)*
Customer	Oh, I see.
You	*(Ask if he wants to hold.)*
Customer	Hmm, I don't think so.
You	*(Ask if he can call back later.)*
Customer	Yes, OK, thank you. Bye.
You	*(Say goodbye.)*

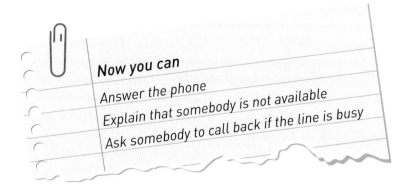

Now you can

Answer the phone

Explain that somebody is not available

Ask somebody to call back if the line is busy

14 Outgoing calls

Asking to speak to somebody | Checking telephone numbers | Thanking people

Telephone calls

1 Jasmine Goodman from Lowis Engineering wants to call three people to check arrangements for meetings. Listen to her side of the telephone conversations. Does she speak to the people she wants to contact?

A

Jasmine

Ah, good morning. **Could I speak to Alan Jay, please?** ... He's in a meeting. OK, I'll call back later. ... Is 12 o'clock OK? ... Great! **Can you give me his extension number, please?** ... 8 – 6 – 5 –1. Well, **many thanks for your help!**

B

Jasmine

Hi, I'd like to speak to Andrea Schmidt, please. ... Hello, Ms Schmidt. **This is Jasmine Goodman calling from** Lowis Engineering. ... **I'm calling about** our meeting next Wednesday in London. **I just want to check** if that is OK for you. ... Good. Well, **thanks very much**, Ms Schmidt. ... See you next week. Goodbye.

C	
Jasmine	Hello, my name's Jasmine Goodman from Lowis Engineering. **Can you put me through to** Mr Johansson, please? ... Oh, on a business trip? ... Um ... can you give me his mobile number, please? ... 00 49 1552 8896441. And can you give me his land line number also? ... I see, so that's 00 49 899 315 96021. ... All right. Well, **thanks a lot**.

Did you know?

A mobile phone in British English is a cell phone in American English.

Generally, in American English you say zero for 0 and 'Oh' in British English.

Understanding

19
CD

2 Listen again and answer the questions.

1 Does Jasmine have Alan's direct telephone number?

2 What reason does Jasmine give for calling Ms Schmidt?

3 Why can't Mr Johansson speak to Jasmine?

Key phrases

Making telephone calls

Could I speak to XYZ, please?	I'm calling about ... .
Hi, I'd like to speak to XYZ, please.	I just want to check ... .
This is XYZ calling from	Many thanks for your help!
Can you give me his extension number, please?	Thanks very much.
	Thanks a lot.
Can you put me through to ...?	

Practice

3 Match the questions and statements to the replies.

1 Can you give me his extension?   A My pleasure.

2 Well, thanks very much!   B What time today?

3 Could I speak to Ms Kennedy?   C It's 4155.

4 I'd like to speak to Mr White.   D Hi, Paul!

5 I'm calling about our meeting today.   E I'll put you through to him.

6 This is Paul Rogers calling from APU.   F I'm afraid she's in a meeting.

4 Put the words in the sentences into the correct order.

1 you to Can me through put James please Harris,

_____?

2 calling month about I'm the conference next

_____.

3 I number flight want to check just your

_____.

4 you mobile give Mr Can Carter's me number

_____?

5 I Please speak to could White Kate

_____?

6 Anthony much very Well, thanks

_____.

🔊 20 CD **5** Jasmine phones Anton White in Paris to check if he is coming to the meeting at Lowis Engineering. Put the sentences into the correct order to make a conversation. Then listen to Track 20 to check.

1	Jasmine	Could I speak to Mr White, please?
	White	Hello, Jasmine.
	Jasmine	Oh, good! Well, thanks a lot, Mr White and see you next week. Bye.
	White	Anton White.
	Jasmine	Hi Mr White, this is Jasmine Goodman calling from Lowis Engineering.
	Jasmine	I'm just calling about the meeting next Tuesday at 10 o'clock. I just want to check if the time is OK for you.
	Receptionist	I'll put you through.
	White	The time is fine. No problem at all.
	Jasmine	Bye.
	White	See you then. Bye.

Language tip

Say telephone numbers individually, for example, 3156 is *three one five six*. Two numbers the same are given either individually or with the word *double*, for example, 004 is *zero zero four* or *double oh four*. 55 is *double 5*.

If you want to end a telephone conversation, use the word *Well* followed by a *thank you* to let the person you are speaking to know that you have finished, for example, *Well, many thanks for your help!* or *All right. Well, thanks a lot!*

Speaking

 6 You want to try to call your contact at a hotel to arrange a meeting. Play
21-22   Track 21 and speak after the beep. Then listen to Track 22 to compare
CD   your conversation.

Receptionist	Apelles Hotels, how can I help you?
You	*(Give your name and company and ask to speak to Cindy Fox.)*
Receptionist	I'll put you through. ... Oh, I'm sorry she's on a business trip.
You	*(Ask for Ms Fox's mobile phone number.)*
Receptionist	Yes, of course. It's 0155 289 6645.
You	*(Repeat the number, thank the receptionist and say goodbye.)*
Receptionist	Goodbye.

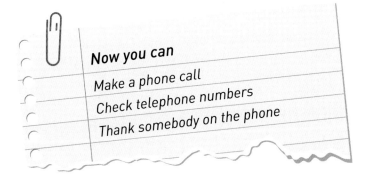

Now you can

Make a phone call

Check telephone numbers

Thank somebody on the phone

15   When things go wrong

Checking deliveries | Dealing with delivery problems | Asking for information

Telephone calls

◀)) **1**   Jasmine Goodman has to make a phone call to a catering supplier, Benji's,
23   and to a package delivery company, TPS. What are the two problems?
CD

A Benji's	Benji's Catering, can I help you?
Jasmine	Yeah, this is Jasmine Goodman from Lowis Engineering. I'm calling about an order for food I made for today.
Benji's	Yes?
Jasmine	**There's a problem with** the lunchtime special executive menu for ten I ordered. **You sent the wrong delivery**.
Benji's	What did you receive?
Jasmine	Er, let me see the delivery note. Ah yes, the children's party special.
Benji's	Ah, I see.
Jasmine	**Could you pick it up** from our office?
Benji's	Yes, of course.
Jasmine	And **can you give us a refund**, please? We really don't need the lunch special now.

B TPS	Thank you for calling TPS. To arrange a pickup, press 1. For the latest information on a package sent with TPS, press 2.
Tony	TPS, good morning. This is Tony speaking, how can I help you?
Jasmine	Oh, hi. My name's Jasmine Goodman. **It's concerning** a package I sent to Singapore. **Something's gone wrong with** the delivery. It hasn't arrived yet.
Tony	OK. Can I have your tracking number, please?
Jasmine	Er, it's MU 76344 HJ.
Tony	Let me just check for you. ... Yes, sorry to keep you waiting. I'm afraid it's been delayed. It's in the Singapore depot at the moment. Apparently, there was a problem with the delivery address.
Jasmine	Oh, really? **What's happened to** it?
Tony	It seems the house number didn't exist. Can I check it with you? Was it to 40 Golden Orchard Road?
Jasmine	No, 14!
Tony	Right – one four. I see.
Jasmine	**Can you tell me when it'll be delivered?**
Tony	We'll put it on a truck right away so it will arrive today. I sincerely apologize for any inconvenience.

Did you know?

With automated phone menus you sometimes press the *hash (#)*, *pound (£)* or *star (*)* keys.

Understanding

23
CD

2 Listen again to the two conversations. Are the sentences true (T) or false (F)?

1 Jasmine didn't make an order to Benji's Catering.   T / F
2 Jasmine wants Benji's to pick up the order.   T / F
3 Jasmine wants money back from Benji's.   T / F
4 Jasmine is waiting for a package from Singapore.   T / F
5 The package is still in London.   T / F
6 TPS had the wrong address.   T / F

Key phrases

Describing problems and asking for information

There's a problem with	Could you collect it / pick it up ... ?
It's concerning	Can you give us a refund?
You sent the wrong delivery / order.	What's happened to ... ?
Something's gone wrong with	Can you tell me when it'll be delivered?

Practice

3 Join the two parts of the sentences together.

1	Something's gone wrong	A	to our order?
2	What's happened	B	the delivery.
3	Can you give	C	up the package?
4	There's a problem with	D	with the reservation.
5	Could you pick	E	me a refund?

4 Put the words in the sentences into the correct order.

1 you package me when Can you will collect the tell

_____?

2 equipment our order concerning for It's office

_____.

3 the delivered wrong with package Something is you

_____.

4 my concerning LO 743 KL package, tracking It's number

_____.

5 our happened to What's delivery

_____?

6 sent to the company wrong You delivery our

_____.

5 Complete the sentences on the left that go with the response on the right. Use the Key phrases box to help you.

1	_____ arrive?	The truck is on its way to you now, sir.
2	Can you _____?	Yes, of course. How much did you pay?
3	_____ it up?	No problem. When is a good time?
4	What's _____?	Can I have your tracking number, please?
5	_____ wrong _____.	Oh, what did we send?

Language tip

24
CD

Be careful when giving the following numbers to a business partner. They frequently cause problems. Listen to the pairs.

13 – 30   14 – 40   15 – 50   16 – 60   17 – 70   18 – 80   19 – 90

Make sure your pronunciation is clear, and, if you are not sure what your partner says, check carefully to avoid mistakes.

24
CD

Here is a way to remember how to pronounce similar sounding letters of the alphabet in English. Listen to the letters.

A H J K

B C D E G P T V Z (US)

F L M N S X Z (UK)

I Y

O

Q U W

R

Speaking

5–26
CD

6 You call a supplier to complain about a delivery. Play Track 25 and speak after the beep. Then listen to Track 26 to compare your conversation.

Supplier	Jackson Office Supplies. How can I help you?
You	*(Give your name and company. Say you have a problem with an order you made last week.)*
Supplier	I'm sorry to hear that. Can you give me the order number?
You	*(JYG 723 / 19 / BP. Say they sent the wrong ink for the printers.)*
Supplier	Oh, I see.
You	*(Ask them to pick up the wrong ink and bring the right ink – TP2000.)*
Supplier	No problem.
You	*(Ask when they will come.)*
Supplier	I think tomorrow should be possible. Is that OK?
You	*(Say that's OK and goodbye.)*

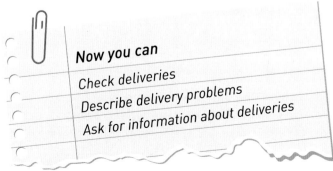

Now you can

Check deliveries

Describe delivery problems

Ask for information about deliveries

16 Telephone messages

Taking messages | Leaving messages | Confirming information

Telephone calls

1 Jasmine Goodman has to answer her boss's telephone this week. Listen to extracts from three telephone conversations. Where is Diane?

A	Jasmine	Jasmine Goodman.
	Alan	Good morning, Jasmine. This is Alan Jay from Texas Consultants. I'd like to speak to Diane Kennedy, please.
	Jasmine	I'm afraid she's away this week, Mr Jay. **Can I take a message**?
	Alan	Yes. Can you tell her I'm flying to London next week and I'll see her at the sales conference?
	Jasmine	**Can I just check that?** You're coming to London next week and you'll see her at the sales conference.
	Alan	Yes, that's right.
B	Jasmine	Hello, Jasmine Goodman.
	Tina	Hi, Tina Jones here, Jasmine. Can I speak to Diane, please?
	Jasmine	I'm sorry, Ms Jones, but she's not here. She's back on Monday next week.

Tina	OK. Well, **could you take a message?**
Jasmine	Yes, of course.
Tina	Tell her I can come to the meeting on the 14th and that my colleague, Marco Toncini, is coming too. But we won't get to you until 10 o'clock. Our flight from Milan only arrives at 8.30.
Jasmine	All right, **let me repeat that**: you and Mr Toncini will be at the meeting on the 14th from 10 o'clock. Is there anything else I can help you with?

C

Jasmine	Jasmine Goodman.
Mark	Hello, Jasmine. It's Mark Pole here.
Jasmine	Hi, Mark.
Mark	Is Diane in the office?
Jasmine	She's on holiday this week, Mark. **Do you want to leave a message for her?**
Mark	Well, you can tell her I called, but I also want to send her an email. Could you give me her email address?
Jasmine	Yes, of course. It's diane.kennedy@lowis-engineering.com.
Mark	**I'll read that back to you**: diane dot kennedy at lowis hyphen engineering dot com.
Jasmine	Right. And I'll tell her you called.

Did you know?

In email addresses, '@' is at, '-' is hyphen, '.' is dot and '_' is underscore.

Understanding

2 Listen again and find the mistakes in the messages Jasmine writes for Diane.

27 CD

Telephone message 1
From: Alan Jay   To: Diane Kennedy
Mr Jay is flying to Liverpool next month and will see you at the sales conference.

Telephone message 2
From: Tina James   To: Diane Kennedy
Ms James is coming to the meeting on the 4th with her colleague Marco Toncini. She'll arrive at 10 o'clock.

Telephone message 3
From: Mark Pole   To: Diane Kennedy
Mark called. He is sending you something in the post.

Key phrases

Taking and leaving a message

Can I take a message?	*Can I just check that?*
Could you take a message?	*Let me repeat that: ...*
Do you want to leave a message for her?	*I'll read that back to you: ...*

Practice

3 Put the words in the sentences into the correct order.

1 Can for I Carter leave message a Mr

_____?

2 you me message like to leave him Would a

_____?

3 message read you the back I'll to

_____.

4 take you Goodman a message Could for Jasmine

_____?

5 I information just check Can the

_____?

6 Rogers want you leave a Do message for Mr to

_____?

4 John Carter wants Jasmine to give Diane a message. Listen to Track 28 and complete the form.

28
CD

Telephone message

From: John Carter   To: Diane Kennedy

Date: May 4

_____

_____

_____

Language tip

Don't be afraid to repeat something back if you are not sure you have the right information. Speak slowly and clearly, especially when you repeat back numbers and names.

Speaking

5 A customer calls you to speak to your boss. You have to take a message. Play Track 29 and speak after the beep. Then listen to Track 30 to compare your conversation.

29–30
CD

Customer	Can I speak to Mr Rogers, please?
You	*(Say you're sorry but he's in a meeting.)*
Customer	Oh, I see. I have some information for him.
You	*(Ask if you can take a message.)*
Customer	Um...yes, OK. Can you tell him that my conference in June is cancelled? If he wants to speak to me about it, he can call me on my new mobile. The number is 01521 300 9957.
You	*(Say that you want to check the information. Repeat the information and the mobile phone number.)*
Customer	That's right. Thanks very much. Goodbye.
You	*(Say goodbye.)*

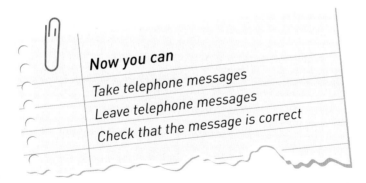

Now you can
Take telephone messages
Leave telephone messages
Check that the message is correct

17 Conference arrangements

Reserving a meeting room | Checking equipment | Arranging refreshments

Telephone call

🔊 **1** Jasmine wants to organize a large business meeting in a hotel. Listen to
31   her phone call. Where will the participants eat lunch?
CD

Cindy	Apelles Hotel Reservation Department, Cindy Fox speaking. How can I help you?
Jasmine	Good morning. My name's Jasmine Goodman. **I'd like to reserve a room for a** meeting from 9 o'clock until 6 o'clock for next Friday, April 27th.
Cindy	Are you a customer of ours already, Ms Goodman?
Jasmine	Yes. It's Lowis Engineering.
Cindy	All right. How many participants will there be?
Jasmine	20 to 25.
Cindy	OK, let me check. ... Yes, that's fine, Ms Goodman. The Napoleon and the Wellington Suites are both available.
Jasmine	Excellent. I'd like the Wellington Suite, please. Now, **does the room have a** projector?
Cindy	Yes, and Internet. Is there anything else you need?
Jasmine	**Could you provide a** flipchart and four pinboards?

Cindy	Yes.
Jasmine	Good. Now, **can you set up a coffee break** for 10.15, and another break for 4.30, please?
Cindy	OK. What about water and juice during the meeting?
Jasmine	Oh, good idea! Next, lunch: **Please could you reserve tables in the hotel restaurant** for 1 o'clock?
Cindy	Certainly, Ms Goodman.
Jasmine	Good. Now, **would you mind repeating that back to me**?
Cindy	Of course. Friday 27th, the Wellington Suite from 9.00 until 6.00 for 20 to 25 people. Coffee at 10.15, lunch at one, and a coffee break again at 4.30, plus water and juice in the meeting room.
Jasmine	And **don't forget the** equipment!
Cindy	One projector, one flipchart and three pinboards.
Jasmine	No. One projector, one flipchart and four pinboards.
Cindy	Sorry, got that. I'll confirm it all in an email to you.
Jasmine	Thanks. My email address is ... .

Did you know?

A pinboard in British English is called *a bulletin board* in American English.

Understanding

2   Listen again. Are the sentences true (T) or false (F)?

1   Jasmine wants to reserve a room for a conference.   T / F
2   The Wellington Suite has a projector for presentations.   T / F
3   Jasmine doesn't want any other presentation equipment.   T / F
4   Jasmine arranges an afternoon break for 3.30 pm.   T / F
5   The meeting will last all day.   T / F

Key phrases

Making a hotel reservation for a meeting

I'd like to reserve / book a room for a	*Please could you reserve / book tables in the hotel restaurant?*
Does the room have a ... ?	*Would you mind repeating that back to me?*
Could you provide a ... ?	
Can you organize / set up a coffee break for ... ?	*Don't forget the ... .*

3 Complete the sentences with words from the box.

reserve	forget	mind	projector	provide

1 Can you set up a _____ in the room?
2 Could you _____ coffee and tea at about 4 o'clock?
3 Would you _____ repeating that back to me?
4 I'd like to _____ a conference room, please.
5 Don't _____ the pinboards!

4 Put the words in the sentences into the correct order.

1 you tables us reserve Please could some for

_____?

2 like I'd to reserve tickets some

_____.

3 you me repeating Would that to mind back, please

_____?

4 the connection room Does have Internet an

_____?

5 organize next a meeting you Can for week

_____?

5 Play Track 32 and listen to another customer speaking to Cindy Fox.
Complete the reservation form.

32
CD

Apelles Reservation Form

Customer name: _____ Company: Topaz Lighting

Date: _____ Time: _____

Meeting room: Napoleon Suite

Participant numbers: _____

Equipment required: _____

Refreshments: Coffee break +

Time required: _____

Language tip

When you are calling to make a reservation, use *I'd like to reserve...* . Then to make any particular requests, use *Could you ... ?* or *Can you ... ?*, for example, *Could you provide tea and coffee?*

When making arrangements over the phone, it is always worth asking for written confirmation, for example, *Could you confirm the details in an email?*

Speaking

6 You are calling Cindy Fox to make a reservation for your company. Play Track 33 and speak after the beep. Then listen to Track 34 to compare your conversation.

33-34
CD

Hotel Apelles Hotel reservation department, Cindy Fox speaking. How can I help you?

You *(Give your name and company. Say you want to reserve a meeting room for July 30, 10.00 – 3.00.)*

Hotel All right. For how many participants?

You *(Say 14.)*

Hotel Yes, that's fine. The Napoleon Suite is available.

You *(Ask if the room has an Internet connection.)*

Hotel Yes, it does. Is there anything else you need?

You *(Ask if the hotel could provide a multimedia projector and flip chart.)*

Hotel No problem. What about refreshments?

You *(Say you would like sandwiches and coffee at 12.00.)*

Hotel Fine. I'll confirm this in an email.

You *(Say thanks and goodbye.)*

Now you can

Telephone a hotel to make a reservation

Confirm presentation equipment

Arrange refreshments

18 Travel plans

Arranging a meeting | Checking availability | Agreeing a convenient time

Telephone call

🔊 **1** Jasmine Goodman wants to make an appointment for her boss, Diane
35   Kennedy, with Peter Wasilewski in Gdansk next week. Jasmine phones
CD   him. Listen to the conversation. When do they set up the meeting for?

Jasmine	Diane is flying to Warsaw the day after tomorrow and visiting Gdansk next week. **Would it be possible for her to see you** then, Mr Wasilewski?
Peter	Hmm, I'm quite busy, but I'm sure we can find time.
Jasmine	I see. **Do you have time on** Tuesday afternoon at 2 pm?
Peter	Er, no. I'm afraid I have a meeting from 2 until 6 o'clock.
Jasmine	OK. Well, **would Wednesday morning be convenient** for you?
Peter	Ah, I'm sorry but I have an appointment at the dentist at 9.00. Is Ms Kennedy available on the day after? I mean Thursday?
Jasmine	Oh sorry, no, I'm afraid not. She has to be back in London by noon on Thursday. **Are you available on** Wednesday afternoon?
Peter	Hmm, let me see. Yes, I can do that.
Jasmine	Excellent! So, **could you meet Ms Kennedy at** 2.30 in your office? **Does that work for you?**

Peter	Yes, that's fine. I look forward to seeing her then.
Jasmine	Thanks very much. I'll tell her. Bye.
Peter	Bye.

Did you know?

Use *Ms* for both married and unmarried women, or *Mrs* for married women. There is no similar distinction for men in English. It is always *Mr*.

Understanding

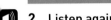

2 Listen again and choose the best answer A, B or C for each question.

35
CD

1 Peter Wasilewski's office is in:

   A London

   B Warsaw

   C Gdansk

2 Mr Wasilewski's Tuesday afternoon meeting finishes:

   A at some time before 6.00

   B at 6.00

   C after 6.00

3 Diane is coming back to London:

   A no later than 12.00 on Thursday

   B not before 12.00 on Thursday

   C on Thursday afternoon

Key phrases

Asking for an appointment

Would it be possible for her to see you then / on ... / at ... ?	*Are you / Is she available tomorrow / on Thursday?*
Do you have time on Friday / next Tuesday?	*Could you meet her at 4.30?*
Would Monday / Thursday be convenient for you?	*Does that work for you?*

Practice

3 Join the two parts of the sentences together.

1	Are you available	a	11.30?
2	Would Tuesday morning	b	time on Friday?
3	Could you meet Mr Carter at	c	on Tuesday morning?
4	Would it be possible for	d	Mr Rogers to see you?
5	Do you have	e	be convenient for you?

4 Put the words in the questions into the correct order.

1 10.30 you Does work for

_____?

2 Would Kennedy lunchtime, be you convenient Ms for

_____?

3 be it possible Would for him to me see tomorrow

_____?

4 John morning available on Is Monday

_____?

5 you to Jasmine meet quarter at Could four

_____?

5 Jasmine phones Eva Miskiewicz in Warsaw to make another appointment for Diane. Put the sentences into the correct order to make a conversation. Then listen to Track 36 to check.

36
CD

1	Jasmine	... Diane will be flying to Warsaw on Monday. Do you have time on Monday?
	Eva	Sure. That would be fine.
	Jasmine	Well, are you available on Monday evening? Ms Kennedy would like to take you to dinner.
	Eva	Well, after 10.00 perhaps.
	Eva	That's very kind, but I have another appointment in the evening.
	Eva	On Monday? Hmm, that's difficult.
	Jasmine	Mmm, well, would Tuesday morning be convenient for you?
	Jasmine	Great! How about 11 o'clock? Does that work for you?

Language tip

Use *until* to describe a complete period of time during which an action takes place, for example, *I've got a meeting from 2 until 6 o'clock.* = The meeting starts at 2.00 and finishes at 6.00.

Use *by* to set the latest point when an action has to take place, for example, *She has to be back in London by noon on Thursday.* = 12.00 Thursday is the latest time when Diane must be back in the office in London.

Speaking

6 You are calling a customer to arrange a time for a meeting. Play Track 37 and speak after the beep. Then listen to Track 38 to compare your conversation.

7–38
CD

Customer	So you are flying to Madrid next week? Hmm, when can we meet?
You	*(Ask if he is free on Tuesday.)*
Customer	Tuesday? No sorry, I'm away on a business trip.
You	*(Ask about Wednesday morning.)*
Customer	I'm afraid Wednesday morning is no good. I have to go to the doctor.
You	*(Ask about Wednesday afternoon.)*
Customer	Um ... yes ... I think so.
You	*(Suggest 3 o'clock.)*
Customer	Is a little later possible?
You	*(Suggest 4 o'clock at the latest because you have to leave by 6.00.)*
Customer	Yes, that's fine. I'll see you then!

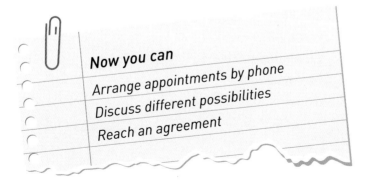

Now you can
Arrange appointments by phone
Discuss different possibilities
Reach an agreement

19 Welcome back

Greeting people you know | Giving a gift | Thanking somebody for a gift

Conversation

DVD

1 John Carter and Paul Rogers return to Lowis Engineering. Jasmine comes down to reception to meet them. Read their conversation and watch the video. Why does Paul give Jasmine a present?

Jasmine	Jasmine Goodman. Hello, Sally. ... John Carter and Paul Rogers? Yes, that's fine. I'll come and get them. ... Great, thanks very much, Sally.
Paul	Jasmine, **good to see you again**!
Jasmine	Hello, Paul. Hi, John. **Nice to see you again too**!
John	**How are you**, Jasmine?
Jasmine	**I'm fine, thanks. And you?**
John	**Very well, thanks**.
Jasmine	Have you checked into your hotel OK?
John	Yes, we have.
Jasmine	Good, good.
Paul	Thank you for organizing everything for us again.
Jasmine	No problem.

Paul	And **this is a small present from our company** to say thank you for all your help.
Jasmine	**... Oh, thank you very much! That's really kind of you!**
Paul	No worries.
Jasmine	I'll open it upstairs. Ready to go up?
Paul	Yeah.

Did you know?

In some cultures it is impolite to open a present or gift immediately.

Understanding

DVD

2 Watch again. Are the sentences true (T) or false (F)?

1	John and Paul come up to Jasmine's office by themselves.	T / F
2	Jasmine knows John and Paul already.	T / F
3	John and Paul needed to make a hotel reservation.	T / F
4	Jasmine is pleased with her present from John and Paul.	T / F
5	Jasmine opens her present immediately.	T / F

Key phrases

Greeting acquaintances, giving and receiving a gift

Good to see you again!	*Very well, thanks.*
Nice to see you again too!	*This is a small present from ... .*
How are you?	*Thank you very much! That's really kind*
I'm fine, thanks. And you? / How about you?	*of you.*

Practice

3 Match the sentences.

1	That's really kind of you!	A	Thank you very much. It's lovely!
2	How are you?	B	Nice to see you again too!
3	Good to see you again!	C	Fine thanks, Jasmine. And you?
4	This is a gift from our country.	D	You're welcome.

4 Put the words in the sentences into the correct order.

1 really you kind That's of

_____.

2 to again Diane see you Nice too,

_____.

3 Tony are How you,

_____?

4 a us small of present from Here's all

_____.

5 thanks. about you And Fine, how

_____?

5 Read the conversation between Jasmine and Jon Martin from Anchor Hotels. In each numbered line there is a small mistake. Find and correct it.

1	Jon	Hello Jasmine. Good too see you again! _____
2	Jasmine	Hello, Jon. Nice to see you again to! _____
3	Jon	How is you? _____
4	Jasmine	Fine, thank. And you? _____
5	Jon	Very while, thanks. _____
	Jasmine	Good.
6	Jon	Thanks four using Anchor Hotels for your conference. _____
7	Jasmine	Mine pleasure. _____
8	Jon	And these is a small present from Anchor Hotels. _____
9	Jasmine	Oh, thank you very much! That are really kind of you! _____
10	Jon	Not it all. _____

Language tip

When somebody thanks you, use one of the following replies:
My pleasure.
You're welcome!
Not at all!
No worries. (Informal)

Speaking

6 You are meeting Colin, a colleague from another country, at your company. Play Track 39 and speak after the beep. Then listen to Track 40 to compare your conversation.

9–40
CD

Colin	Hello! Good to see you again!
You	*(Reply.)*
Colin	How are you?
You	*(Say you're fine and ask about him)*
Colin	Very well. And thank you so much for arranging my hotel room.
You	*(Reply.)*
Colin	And here is a small thank-you present for all your hard work.
You	*(Reply.)*
Colin	My pleasure!

Now you can
Greet people you know
Give a gift
Thank somebody for a gift

20 Plans

Explaining a schedule | Describing a sequence of events | Talking about future plans

Conversation

 1 Jasmine has put together a schedule for John Carter and Paul Rogers.
DVD   Read their conversation and watch the video. Who has John met before?

Jasmine	So, here's the schedule for the next two days. Can I just run through it?
John	Yes, of course.
Jasmine	All right. **First of all,** this afternoon you're meeting Chris Fox, the factory manager, together with Diane. They want to show you the factory.
Paul	Interesting.
Jasmine	**After** Chris has given you the tour, Diane wants to show you some of our ideas for the new equipment and you can talk to some of our engineers. **And then** Diane is taking you to dinner, together with Mr Harris, the Managing Director of Lowis Engineering.
John	Sounds good.
Jasmine	**Next,** tomorrow morning at 9.30, Diane and I are picking you up from your hotel to take you by car to our test facility just outside of London and you can see some of our equipment in action.
Paul	That'll be interesting.

Jasmine	I hope so. **While** you're there, you're meeting the test manager, Jim Gibson, and he can show you everything.
John	Great, I know Jim already, in fact.
Jasmine	Ah, good. **Finally**, at about 4 o'clock a taxi's picking you up from here and taking you to the airport. Your flight back to Australia is at 7 o'clock, I think.
Paul	Yes, that's right. Well, that all sounds very well organized. Thanks again, Jasmine.
Jasmine	You're welcome.

Understanding

DVD

2 Watch again and complete the schedule below for John and Paul.

Today
11.00 am – _arrive Lowis Engineering_ _____
1.00 pm _____
3.00 pm _____
6.00 pm _____

Tomorrow
9.30 am _____
4.00 pm _____
7.00 pm – _flight to Sydney_ _____

Key phrases

Outlining a schedule

First of all, ...	Next, ...
After / After that	While ... .
And then	Finally, ...

3 Complete this article about how to run a successful meeting using the words in the box below.

after	finally	first	next	then	while

Did you know that the average business person sits in meetings for 190 hours every year? That's eight days! So how can you organize effective meetings? (1) _____ of all, think: is a meeting necessary? (2) _____ you have decided it is necessary, don't invite too many people. More than seven and good discussion is difficult. (3) _____ you must plan the agenda carefully and (4) _____ send it in time for people to prepare. (5) _____ the meeting is running, make sure that there is coffee and water for everybody. (6) _____, check that everybody has ... .

4 Put the words in the sentences into the correct order.

1 I'm to Today listen to to my, English work CD while planning driving

_____.

2 all, meeting we're having First a of

_____.

3 that, I'm lunch with having After Jasmine

_____.

4 writing for boss Then a report, I'm my

_____.

5 this a evening I'm going to Finally, movie

_____.

5 Look at your diary for next week and write down your plans.

First of all, on Monday I'm _____.

After / After that, on Tuesday _____.

And then on Tuesday afternoon _____.

Next, on Wednesday _____.

Finally, on Friday _____.

Language tip

Use the present continuous tense to talk about definite future plans, for example, *This afternoon you're meeting Chris Fox.*

See page 149 for more information on the present continuous.

Speaking

6 Your manager wants you to explain her schedule for tomorrow with an important customer, Ms Sahdi. Use the diary below to help you. Play Track 41 and speak after the beep. Then listen to Track 42 to compare your conversation.

41–42
CD

Tomorrow
10.00 am – *pick up Ms Sahdi at airport, show her the new office*
11.00 am – *meeting Ms Sahdi, you and sales team*
1.00 pm – *take Ms Sahdi to lunch*
3.00 pm – *visit factory and explain about new equipment*
7.00 pm – *go to theatre and have dinner*

Manager Ah, there you are. Can you tell me about my schedule for tomorrow with Ms Sahdi?

You *(First of all, at 10.00 you're picking up Ms Sahdi at the airport and … .)*

Manager I see. What next?

You *(Next, at 11.00 … .)*

Manager Very well. And then?

You *(And then, … .)*

Manager I see. After that?

You *(After that, … .)*

Manager Good! Anything else?

You *(Finally, … .)*

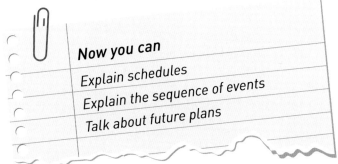

Now you can

Explain schedules

Explain the sequence of events

Talk about future plans

21 A change of plan

Changing arrangements | Apologizing | Giving reasons for changes

Conversation

DVD

1 Jasmine has put together a schedule for John Carter and Paul Rogers. Read their conversation and watch the video. What's the problem?

Jasmine	... and I think that Diane can explain that later. Just a moment! ... Jasmine Goodman ... Oh, hello Diane ... yes, John and Paul are here already ... Oh dear! ... Right ...Yes ... . I'll tell them ... No, don't worry. Yes ... yes .... No problem ... OK ... Well, I hope she's better soon. ... Right, bye ... . Bye.
John	Is there a problem?
Jasmine	Yes, **I'm afraid there is.** That was Diane. Her daughter's sick.
Paul	Nothing serious, I hope?
Jasmine	No, I don't think so but she does need to take her to the doctor. I **truly apologize** but she can't come around the factory with you today. So **we need to adjust the schedule** because she really wants to do that with you.
John	OK.
Jasmine	So **I want to move forward** the visit to our test facility that we planned for tomorrow, to today ...
John	All right.

Jasmine	... and **move back** the visit to the factory to tomorrow so Diane can come as well. **She sends her apologies for changing the plan.**
Paul	No problem. And ... at dinner this evening? Will you come as well, or is it just Mr Harris?
Jasmine	Just Mr Harris. **I'd love to come but** unfortunately I have to babysit for a friend this evening. **I'm really sorry!**

Did you know?

Use *to move* or *bring forward* in British English or *move up* in American English to say that something will be done earlier than planned. In British English, *to move back* or *put back* means to do something at a later time or date.

Understanding

2   Watch the video again. What changes does Jasmine make to the schedule?

Today	Tomorrow
11.00 am – *tour factory with Diane and Chris Fox* 1.00 pm – *sandwiches in office* 3.00 pm – *meet sales team* 6.00 pm – *dinner with Diane and Mr Harris*	9.30 am – *visit test facility. Meet Jim Gibson* 4.00 pm – *taxi from Lowis Engineering to airport* 7.00 pm – *flight to Sydney*

Key phrases

Apologizing	Changing arrangements
I'm afraid there's a problem.	*We need to adjust the schedule / change the plan.*
I truly apologize but	
She sends her apologies for	*I want to move / bring forward (UK)/ move up (US)... . [←]*
I'd love to XYZ but	
I'm so sorry. / I'm so sorry for	*I want to move back / put back (UK) ... . [→]*

Practice

3   Join the two parts of the sentences together.

1   They send their apologies   A   up the meeting.
2   The boss wants to move   B   but we're away on vacation.
3   I need to   C   back the flight by two hours.
4   We'd love to   D   for the delay.
5   The airline has put   E   adjust the schedule.

4 Put the words in the sentences into the correct order.

1 salesteam telephone want bring The conference call forward to the

_____.

2 I for hotel truly the problems with apologize the

_____.

3 I'm afternoon there's the change to a timetable afraid this

_____.

4 sent apologies his He for delay the

_____.

5 so presentation sorry we put I'm the to tomorrow back

_____.

5 Complete the sentences with words from the box.

| truly   sorry   up   back   need   afraid |

1 I'm _____ there's a problem with the flight.
2 I'm so _____ you had to wait.
3 I _____ apologize for the delay.
4 We _____ to change the schedule.
5 I'm moving _____ the meeting from 4 to 3.
6 I'm putting _____ the visit from 3 to 4.

Language tip

If you want someone to understand that something is important, use the auxiliary verb *do*, or emphasizing words like *truly*, *really* or *so*.

She **does** need to take her to the doctor.
She **really** wants to do that with you.
I **truly** apologize.
I'm **so** sorry.

Speaking

6 You have to telephone an important customer, Ms Sahdi, about some changes to the schedule for April 7 that you sent her. Use the diary below to help you. Play Track 43 and speak after the beep. Then listen to Track 44 to compare your conversation.

43–44
CD

Ms Sahdi's schedule, Tuesday – April 7
10.00 am – *met by Mr King at the airport, show her the new office*
11.00 am – *meeting with Mr King and sales team*
 1.00 pm – *lunch in restaurant*
 3.00 pm – *visit factory and see new equipment*
 7.00 pm – *theatre and dinner*

Ms Sahdi	You need to make some changes to the schedule for tomorrow? No problem. Tell me.
You	*(Apologize because Mr King is sick. You will pick her up from the airport.)*
Ms Sahdi	I see.
You	*(Bring forward the visit to the factory to 11 o'clock.)*
Ms Sahdi	I see. After that?
You	*(Apologize that you want to cancel lunch in a restaurant. Sandwiches in the office after the factory visit.)*
Ms Sahdi	That's fine. I don't eat lunch normally. Any other changes?
You	*(Move back the meeting with the sales team to 3 o'clock.)*
Ms Sahdi	That's a good idea. And in the evening?
You	*(Tell her you are taking her to the theatre and then to dinner.)*

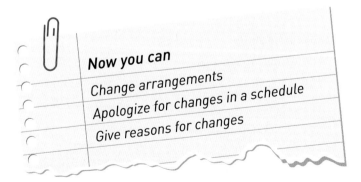

Now you can
Change arrangements
Apologize for changes in a schedule
Give reasons for changes

22 How was your visit?

Asking about past events | Answering questions about the past | Asking opinions

Conversation

DVD

1 Jasmine asks John Carter and Paul Rogers about what they did yesterday.
Read their conversation and watch the video. What didn't Paul see?

Jasmine	... and Diane is just in a short meeting with Mr Harris. She'll be here in five minutes to go with us to the factory. But **how was** your visit to our test facility yesterday?
John	**It was** very interesting. We saw a lot.
Jasmine	**Did you** see the new computer centre?
Paul	**Yeah, we did.** Very impressive! **How much did it cost**?
Jasmine	Oh, **it cost** a lot of money! I'm sure Diane knows how much. You can ask her later. **What did you think** of the testing equipment for the pumps?
Paul	**I didn't** see it, I'm afraid. I stayed in the computer centre. But John did.
John	**I thought** it was fantastic. Very important for checking quality.
Jasmine	**How long did you** stay?
Paul	A couple of hours, I guess.

John	It was longer than that, Paul! We stayed at least three hours. And then your Managing Director, Mr Harris, met us and took us to dinner.
Jasmine	**Did you like** the restaurant?
Paul	Yeah, it was great.
Jasmine	How about you, John?
John	Yes, **I liked** it a lot. I can always eat Italian food.

Did you know?

There are small spelling differences between British and American English, for example *centre* (UK) and *center* (US). Another one is *color* (US) and *colour* (UK).

Understanding

2 Watch again and choose the best answer A, B or C for each question.

1 John and Paul:
   A are going to the test facility
   B were at the test facility
   C are at the test facility

2 Paul:
   A tested the pumps
   B thought about the testing equipment
   C was in the computer centre

3 The restaurant was liked by:
   A both of them
   B only Paul
   C only John

Key phrases

Asking opinions

How **was** your visit?	*Did you like the ... ?*
What **did** you **think of** ... ?	

Talking about the past

It **was**	*I didn't see it. / I thought it was ... .*
Did you **see** ...? → Yes, we **did**. / We **saw**	How long **did** you **stay**? → We **stayed** ... .
How much **did** it **cost**? → It **cost**	→ *I liked it a lot / very much.*

3 Complete the sentences with the words in the box.

| did   didn't   emailed   was   was   wasn't   were |

1 I _____ speak to Mr Harris yesterday. He was sick.
2 Jasmine _____ him the report last week.
3 'How long _____ the flight yesterday?' 'It _____ that long. About two hours.'
4 _____ you see Diane this morning?
5 'How long _____ you in the meeting?' 'I think it _____ about three hours.'

4 Put the words in the sentences into the correct order.

1 How spend much did money you

_____?

2 night I the equipment checked last

_____.

3 you yesterday presentation email Paul Did the

_____?

4 did have Where lunch they

_____?

5 Fox did you Chris What show

_____?

5 Complete the sentences using the verb in brackets in the past simple tense.

1 Jasmine _____ (meet) the visitors from reception at 9 o'clock.
2 Diane _____ (not go) to the test facility with John and Paul yesterday.
3 Jasmine _____ (email) the invitation to Mr Cao in March.
4 How long _____ (to be) your flight?
5 When _____ you _____ (check) the equipment?
6 _____ (to be) you at the airport on time?
7 Mr Harris _____ (to have) a meeting with Diane at 9 o'clock.

Language tip

Use the past simple tense to talk about something that happened in the past at a particular time and is now finished, for example, *We stayed at least three hours* or *It cost a lot of money.*

Also, when you want to give your opinion, start your sentence with *I think* or *I thought* (if talking about the past).

See page 150 for more information on the past simple and page 154 for a list of irregular verbs like *cost.*

Speaking

6 It's Friday. Your manager wants to know what you did this week. Answer his questions using the key words below to help you. Play Track 45 and speak after the beep. Then listen to Track 46 to compare your conversation.

5-46
CD

Manager	And can you tell me about this week? What did you do on Monday?
You	*(check / sales figures)*
Manager	I see. What about the sales presentation?
You	*(go / sales presentation / Wednesday)*
Manager	How was it?
You	*(think / excellent)*
Manager	Very good. And did you visit the customer afterwards?
You	*(visit / customer / Thursday)*
Manager	That's fine. Was Paul Rogers there?
You	*(Mr Rogers / not come / meeting)*
Manager	That's too bad.
You	*(What / you / do / this week?)*

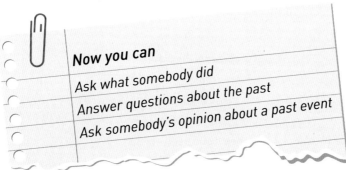

Now you can

Ask what somebody did

Answer questions about the past

Ask somebody's opinion about a past event

23 What can I do for you?

Asking for help | Offering help | Looking after guests

Conversation

 1 Paul needs Jasmine to help him. Read their conversation and watch the
DVD video. How many different things does she do for him?

Paul	Jasmine, can you help me?
Jasmine	Yes, of course. **What can I do for you?**
Paul	I want to print the draft contract from this flash drive.
Jasmine	No problem. **Which document is it?**
Paul	There! The APU and Lowis Engineering contract document.
Jasmine	**Shall I** print one copy or two?
Paul	Er, two please, if that's all right.
Jasmine	Fine. **Would you like me to** staple them together?
Paul	Yeah. Thanks very much.
Jasmine	**There you are. Can I do anything else for you?**
Paul	No. That's all thanks.
Jasmine	Well, **let me know if you need something**.
Paul	All right. Thanks very much, Jasmine. Almost ready.

Jasmine	Ah, good. Thanks. Paul? John's downstairs when you're ready.
Paul	Great. Tell him I'll be with him in a moment.
Jasmine	Yeah. He'll be with him in a moment.

Understanding

ƆVD

2 Watch again. Are the sentences true (T) or false (F)?

1 Paul wants Jasmine to print the final contract.   T / F
2 The contract is on Jasmine's computer.   T / F
3 Paul wants more than one copy of the contract.   T / F
4 Paul doesn't need any more help.   T / F
5 John is waiting for Paul.   T / F

Key phrases

Offering help

What can I do for you?	*There / Here you are.*
Which document / file / folder is it?	*Can I do anything else for you?*
Shall I ... ?	*Let me know if you need something.*
Would you like me to ... ?	

Practice

3 Join the two parts of the sentences together.

1 Would you like   A a car to the airport?
2 Can we do   B he needs anything.
3 Let us know if   C me to call a taxi?
4 Shall I book you   D can I do for you?
5 What   E anything else for Ms Sahdi?

4 Put the words in the sentences into the correct order.

1 we for you arrange Shall a car rental

_____?

2 Cao like presentation Would else anything for Mr his

_____?

3 I do John Can anything else you, for

_____?

4 can do I for What them

_____?

5 Jasmine you something know if Let need

_____.

6 is Which it file

_____?

5 Jasmine needs some help from Sally at reception. Put the sentences into the correct order to make a conversation. Then listen to Track 47 to check.

47
CD

1	Jasmine	Sally, can you help me with something?
	Sally	You're welcome!
	Sally	Sure. What can I do for you?
	Jasmine	Oh, a BMW I think.
	Jasmine	Good idea. Then she can get the keys from you.
	Jasmine	Yes. 9 o'clock is fine.
	Sally	OK. Well, which type of car does she want?
	Jasmine	No, that's all. Thanks a lot.
	Sally	All right, a BMW. Would you like me to ask them to deliver it to the company?
	Jasmine	I need to rent a car for Diane, but I haven't done it before.
	Sally	OK. Can I do anything else for you?
	Sally	No problem. Shall I order one for 9 o'clock?

Language tip

Use *There / Here you are* when you give something to somebody.

Speaking

6 Your manager needs your help with a business trip. Make suggestions. Play Track 48 and speak after the beep. Then listen to Track 49 to compare your conversation.

3-49
CD

Manager	Can you help me?
You	*(Ask what he wants.)*
Manager	I need to fly to London on Thursday morning.
You	*(Offer to make a flight reservation for him.)*
Manager	Oh, thanks very much. And I need a hotel for Thursday and Friday.
You	*(Offer to reserve a room at the Anchor Hotel.)*
Manager	Yeah, that's a nice hotel.
You	*(Ask if he wants anything else.)*
Manager	No, that's all at the moment, thanks.
You	*(Tell him to ask if he needs anything else.)*

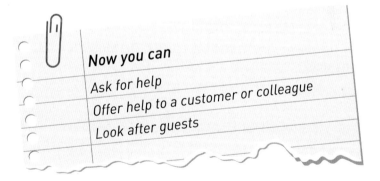

Now you can

Ask for help

Offer help to a customer or colleague

Look after guests

24 Goodbye

Saying goodbye politely | Thanking people | Wishing people a good trip

Conversation

DVD

1   Jasmine is saying goodbye to John and Paul. Read their conversation
    and watch the video. Why does it sometimes take longer to get to the
    airport on Friday?

Jasmine	So, your taxi should be here soon.
John	How long is it from here to the airport?
Jasmine	Oh, only half an hour normally. But on Friday there's sometimes lots of traffic.
Paul	Well, our flight isn't until 7.00, so we have lots of time.
Jasmine	Oh, look, there's the taxi!
John	**Well, goodbye then,** Jasmine.
Jasmine	**Yes, goodbye. It was nice seeing you again**.
Paul	Yeah, and **thanks very much for** organizing everything for us.
Jasmine	My pleasure. **I hope you enjoyed your visit.**
John	Definitely. It was great visiting the factory and seeing the equipment in action.
Jasmine	**Good. I'm glad you enjoyed it.**

John	All right. We must go then.
Jasmine	Yes, the taxi's waiting.
Paul	**So, see you again soon, I hope**.
Jasmine	**Bye, bye. Take care**.
Paul	Thanks, Jasmine. **Bye**.
Jasmine	**Bye. Have a good flight!**

Did you know?

When you say goodbye in English to somebody who is important to you, you very often repeat yourself several times like in the example above. It is unusual to simply say *Bye* and just go. That is seen as unfriendly.

Understanding

2 Watch again and choose the best answer A, B or C for each question.

1 John and Paul's flight leaves:
  A before 7 o'clock in the evening
  B at 7 o'clock in the evening
  C after 7 o'clock in the evening

2 John was:
  A pleased with his visit
  B bored with his visit
  C disappointed with his visit

3 Jasmine says that she hopes John and Paul:
  A are very careful
  B come again soon
  C have a comfortable trip

Key phrases

Saying goodbye

Well, goodbye then.	*Good. I'm glad you enjoyed it.*
Yes, goodbye. It was nice seeing you again.	*So, see you again soon, I hope.*
Thanks very much for … .	*Bye, bye. Take care.*
I hope you enjoyed your visit.	*Bye. Have a good flight!*

Practice

3 Match the sentence on the left with the response on the right.

1	I hope you enjoyed the presentation.	A	I hope so too.
2	Goodbye, take care!	B	My pleasure!
3	So, see you again soon I hope.	C	It was great.
4	Thanks very much for looking after us.	D	Thanks, bye.
5	Bye. Have a good trip.	E	Yeah, you too! Bye.

4 Put the words in the sentences into the correct order.

1 Well, Chen goodbye, Mrs then

_____ .

2 hope We you your enjoyed stay

_____ .

3 glad interesting that your We're visit was

_____ .

4 was again both great seeing It you

_____ .

5 see hope you again So, soon, we

_____ .

6 have flight Goodbye and a home good

_____ !

5 Write a sentence that goes with the response underneath.

1 _____ .

I hope to see you again soon too.

2 _____ .

Definitely. It was a fantastic presentation.

3 _____ .

I'm sure we will. Singapore Airlines is very good!

4 _____ .

Yeah, thanks. Bye, Sally.

5 _____ .

It was nice meeting you again too.

Language tip

When you are thanking someone, make sure you sound enthusiastic about what you did with them. You can use these adjectives to say what you think of something:

It was great / fantastic / wonderful / terrific.

Speaking

6 You are saying goodbye to two visitors to your company. Play Track 50 and speak after the beep. Use the key words to help you. Then listen to Track 51 to compare your conversation.

0–51
CD

Visitor 1	Well, we must go. Goodbye then.
You	*(goodbye / nice / meet / again)*
Visitor 2	Yes, it was. And thanks for making the hotel reservation.
You	*(My pleasure / hope / enjoy / visit)*
Visitor 1	Oh yes, it was great. I learned a lot.
You	*(I / glad / visit / useful)*
Visitor 2	Definitely. So, see you again soon, I hope.
You	*(Yes / hope so / too / have / good / flight / goodbye)*
Visitor 1	Thanks. Bye.
Visitor 2	Bye bye.
You	*(goodbye)*

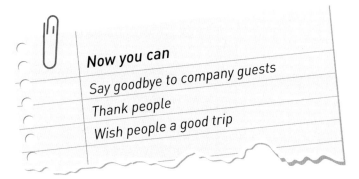

Now you can

Say goodbye to company guests

Thank people

Wish people a good trip

Unit 1 At reception

Conversation

1 John and Paul want to meet Diane Kennedy.

See page 6 for video script.

Understanding

2

1 False. They work at Australian Power Utilities.

2 True

3 True

4 False. They will only have to wait a moment.

Practice

3

1 Good evening, how can I help you?

2 Can I have your names, please?

3 Please could you complete these forms?

4 Someone will come down to get you.

5 Please have a seat.

4

1 B   **2** D   **3** A   **4** C

5

6

Follow model in 5 above.

Speaking

7

Model conversation

You	*Good morning madam, can I help you?*
Guest	Yes, I have an appointment with Diane Kennedy for 11 o'clock.
You	*Can I have your name, please?*
Guest	Jane Taylor from Taylor and Curtiss Consultants.
You	*Right. Can you complete this security form, please?*
Guest	Can you give me a pen?
You	*Here you are.*
Guest	Thanks.
You	*Thank you. And could you wear this visitor badge, please?*
Guest	Of course.
You	*Please have a seat. Someone will come down to get you soon.*
Guest	Good! Thanks for your help!

Lowis Engineering – Visitor Form

Surname / Last name   CARTER
First / Given name   John
Company address   Australian Power Utilities Inc, Block 7 Industrial Park, Canberra
Email   carter@apu.com
Visiting   DIANE KENNEDY
Time in   09:30   Time out _____
Signature *John Carter* _____

Unit 2   Company visitors

Conversation

1   Diane Kennedy asked Jasmine to meet the guests.

See page 10 for video script.

Understanding

2

1   No, they don't.
2   Yes, she does.
3   Yes, they do.
4   Yes, she does.

Practice

3

1   C   2   D   3   E   4   F
5   A   6   B

4

1   I'm John Carter / Paul Rogers and this is my colleague, Paul Rogers / John Carter.
2   We need to take the lift to the 3rd floor.
3   Excuse me, are you Mr Carter?
4   Come this way, please.
5   Mr Carter asked me to meet you.

5

Jasmine	(1) Excuse me, (2) are you Ms Ringwood?
Guest	Yes, that's right.
Jasmine	I'm Jasmine Goodman. (3) Diane Kennedy asked me to meet you.
Guest	Oh, hello Jasmine.
Jasmine	(4) Welcome to Lowis Engineering.
Guest	Thank you!

| Jasmine | This way, please. We (5) need to take the lift to the 3rd floor. |
| Guest | OK. |

Speaking

6

Model conversation

You	*Excuse me, are you Mr Stenson?*
Visitor	Yes, that's right.
You	*Hello. I'm Jan Smith. Mr Brown asked me to meet you. Welcome to our company.*
Visitor	Thank you very much.
You	*Come this way, please. We need take the lift to the 8th floor.*
Visitor	Of course. This is a great building.
You	*Yes, it's a nice place to work.*

Unit 3   What do you do?

Conversation

1   Jasmine has to take the minutes in meetings.

See page 14 for video script.

Understanding

2

1   True
2   False. She usually stays in the office.
3   False. She takes the minutes.
4   True

Practice

3

| 1 | D | 2 | E | 3 | C | 4 | F |
| 5 | B | 6 | A | | | | |

4

| 1 | E | 2 | D | 3 | A | 4 | C | 5 | B |

5

Suggested answers

1   I'm a receptionist / an assistant.
2   I'm responsible for answering the phone.
3   I look after guests.
4   I reply to emails.
5   I deal with inquiries.

Speaking

6

Model conversation

Visitor	So, what do you do?
You	*I'm a sales and marketing assistant.*
Visitor	I see, that's interesting. Are you very busy?
You	*Really busy! The sales team travels a lot and I make all the flight and hotel reservations.*
Visitor	And are you responsible for anything?
You	*I deal with inquiries and send out information about our products.*
Visitor	Do you do anything else?
You	*Yes, I also help to organize the sales conference which is a big job!*

Unit 4   Making visitors feel welcome

Conversation

1 Jasmine calls Paul 'Mr Rogers' to be polite.

See pages 18-19 for video script.

Understanding

2

1 False. They have to wait for her to finish another meeting.
2 True
3 False. He wants some orange juice.
4 True
5 False. They say it's fine and tell Jasmine not to worry.

Practice

3

1 Would you like a cup of tea?
2 I'd like some coffee, please.
3 Would you like to sit down?
4 I'm sorry you have to wait.
5 Mr Carter should be here soon.
6 Would you like milk and sugar?
7 I'm afraid Mrs White is still in a meeting.
8 Here you are.

4

1 B   2 E   3 D   4 A   5 C

5

1 afraid, in
2 like, have / take
3 Here
4 take
5 some / a, please
6 should, soon

Speaking

6

Model conversation

You	Can I take your coats?
Visitor 1	Thank you.
Visitor 2	Here you are.
You	Would you like to sit down?
Visitor 1	Thanks.
You	Would you like some coffee or juice?
Visitor 1	I'd like some coffee, please.
You	What about you, Mr Carter?
Visitor 2	I'd like some orange juice.
You	I'm afraid Ms Kennedy is in a meeting.
Visitor 1	No problem.
You	She should be here soon.
Visitor 2	Thanks.

Unit 5 Small talk

Conversation

1 Diane doesn't arrive for the meeting.

See pages 22–23 for video script.

Understanding

2
1 Frankfurt
2 Jasmine
3 No, they haven't.
4 Tickets for a football match.
5 In a French restaurant.

Practice

3
1 D	2 C	3 B	4 F
5 G	6 E	7 A	

4
1 Is this your first time here?
2 How's your hotel?
3 How was your flight?
4 Do you like the theatre?
5 Would you like to see 'The Lion King'?
6 How long are you staying here?

Speaking

5

Model conversation

You	How was your flight from London?
Visitor	Oh, not very good. The weather in London is terrible at the moment. It's nice to see some sunshine here.
You	Yes, it is. How is the hotel?
Visitor	It's very nice. Thank you for organizing it.
You	My pleasure. Is this your first time here?
Visitor	Yes, this is my first time. What should I do in the evening?
You	Do you like Spanish food?
Visitor	Very much!
You	Would you like to try a local restaurant this evening?
Visitor	Oh, yes! Very much. Thank you.
You	You're welcome. How long are you staying here?
Visitor	Until Friday. Then I fly back to London.
You	Well, I'll check where my boss is and tell him you're here.
Visitor	Thanks a lot.

Unit 6   Introductions

Conversation

1 Because she has already met them.

See page 26 for video script.

Understanding

2

1 False. They have never met Diane before.
2 True
3 True
4 True

Practice

3

1 Nice to meet you, John.
2 This is my colleague, Diane Kennedy.
3 Nice to meet you too.
4 I see you've met my manager, John Carter, already. / I see you've already met my manager, John Carter.
5 Pleased to meet you, Ms Goodman.
6 Please call me Jasmine.

4

1 I'm
2 already
3 is, colleague
4 too
5 like, introduce
6 call

5

[1]	Jasmine	Diane, can I introduce you to Mr Kline?
[2]	Diane	Nice to meet you, Mr Kline.
[3]	Mr Kline	Nice to meet you too. But please call me Mike.
[4]	Diane	Of course. And I'm Diane. Would you like to take a seat?
[5]	Mr Kline	Thank you.
[6]	Diane	And would you like some coffee?
[7]	Mr Kline	No, thanks.
[8]	Diane	So how was your flight?
[9]	Mr Kline	OK, but it was a bit late taking off.

Speaking

6

Model conversation

Colleague	So here we are! I'd like to introduce Lee Toms from DPU.
You	*Nice to meet you, Mr Toms.*
Lee	Nice to meet you too but please call me Lee.
You	*And I'm Sue. Please take a seat.*
Lee	Thank you.
You	*I'm sorry I'm late.*
Lee	No problem.
You	*Would you like some coffee?*
Lee	No, thanks.
You	*How was your journey here?*
Lee	It was fine. No problems.

Unit 7   An inquiry by email

Email
1 Jasmine is writing to Anchor Hotels.

Understanding
2
1 C   2 B   3 A

Practice
3
1 C   2 F   3 A   4 E
5 B   6 D

4
1 Please include your address and telephone number. *Or* Please include your telephone number and address.
2 We would like to invite you to a presentation.
3 I would be grateful if you could send us a brochure.
4 Please let me know if this time is possible for you.
5 I look forward to seeing you on Tuesday.

5
1 I **am** writing / **I'm** writing …
2 … is **organizing** …
3 We **would** like to …
4 … **let me** …
5 I **would** be grateful …
6 Please **include** a …
7 … to **hearing** from you.

Writing
6
Suggested answer
To Whom It May Concern (US English) / Dear Sir or Madam (UK English)

I am writing to ask about meeting facilities in your hotel.
On April 19, Crayton Car Rentals is organizing its Annual General Meeting for about 300 guests. Please let me know if your conference facilities are available on this date.

I would be grateful if you could send me information about room size, presentation equipment, catering facilities and costs.

I look forward to hearing from you.

Best regards (US) / Yours faithfully (UK)

Unit 8   A reply to an inquiry

Email
1 A 25% discount on bookings before the end of February.

Understanding
2
1 False. The conference is for May 3.
2 False. The hotel also supplies a PDF file with information about the hotel.
3 True
4 False. They still have rooms available for May 3.
5 True

Practice

3

1 discount
2 email
3 price information
4 conference facilities
5 contact
6 available

4

1 If you would like further information, contact me on 0207 98 5151.
2 I am pleased to inform you that this date is available.
3 Thank you for your phone call this morning.
4 Please find attached our service information. / Please find our service information attached.
5 With reference to your email of March 27, ...

5

> Dear Ms Goodman
>
> Thank you for your phone call to my assistant this afternoon. [1]
>
> With reference to the date of your event, we have rooms available at that time. [2]
>
> Please find enclosed information about our conference equipment and prices. [3]
>
> We are pleased to inform you that we have a special offer for catering facilities in May. [4]
>
> If you would like further information, please let me know. [5]
>
> Yours sincerely [6]
>
> Priti Makesch

Writing

6

Audio script

Hi! This is Fran here. I'm in a meeting this afternoon. Can you answer the email from John Carter from Australian Power Utilities to say that if he wants to organize a meeting here on March 27th then it's ok? Send him also the price information for the meeting room and presentation equipment and tell him about the 5% discount on catering if he makes a reservation this week. He can call me tomorrow morning if he wants to speak to me. Thanks!

Suggested answer

> Dear Mr Carter
>
> With reference to your email this morning, we have a meeting room available on March 27. Please find enclosed price information for the meeting room and presentation equipment.
>
> I am pleased to inform you that we have a 5% discount for catering if you make a reservation this week. If you would like further information, please contact Ms Stein tomorrow morning.
>
> We look forward to hearing from you.
>
> Yours sincerely

Unit 9   A follow-up email

Email

1   She wants him to arrange three things.

Understanding

2

1   B
2   B
3   C
4   A
5   B

Practice

3

1   E
2   A
3   D
4   B
5   C

4

1   Are you able to come to the meeting tomorrow?
2   Would you mind sending a new contract as soon as possible?
3   Could you send the translation to Paul Rogers?
4   Would you be able to help me?
5   Can you finish the report by Friday?

5

Suggested answers

Could you *write the meeting report*?

Are you able to *go to the meeting on Friday*?

Would you mind *making the hotel/flight/ restaurant reservation*?

Would you be able to *take my calls/my clients to lunch next week*?

Writing

6

1   help
2   show
3   able / available
4   mind
5   advise / let me know

Unit 10 A reply to a follow-up email

Email

1 He makes six suggestions (including sending the photos in the post).

Understanding

2

1 Lunch.
2 A personal card.
3 Because the total price has changed.
4 The photos of the conference rooms.

Practice

3

1 Why don't you arrange a meeting?
2 Would you like me to send an email?
3 Have you tried moving offices?
4 What about changing the time of the meeting?
5 Let me know if you need another date.
6 Should I change the appointment?

4

Suggested answers

1 What about sending an email with the main points?
2 How about writing a brief summary report now?
3 If you like, I could *help you with the figures*.
4 Let me know if you need *any help with anything*.
5 Why don't you leave it until you get back?

5

1 some
2 Why
3 having
4 she
5 organizing
6 to check
7 need

Writing

6

Suggested answer

Dear Sally

Here are some ideas for the office party. Why don't we use the company cafeteria? It's very comfortable. What about starting at 6 pm and finishing at midnight? We need to work the next day!

For music, how about a live band? Would you like me to contact a friend of mine in the band, 'The Big Noise'?

Let me know if you need anything else.

Regards

[your name]

Unit 11   Invitations

Emails

1   A is formal, B is informal.

Understanding

2

1   True
2   False. It is for the afternoon and evening.
3   True
4   False. She also invites Paul.

Practice

3

1   It will be an opportunity for you to meet our Chairman.
2   We would like to invite you to a meeting on Thursday.
3   Would you like to come to lunch?
4   We hope you are able to attend the conference.
5   Are you free at 6 o'clock for a meeting?

4

1   Would you and Sally like to come to dinner on Saturday? / Are you and Sally free for dinner on Saturday?
2   I hope to see you then. / I hope you can come.
3   Best wishes

Writing

5

Suggested answer

Dear Mr Probst

I am writing on behalf of Ms Timms, Sales Director for CMCX Ltd. We would like to invite you to a meeting on Thursday April 7 from 10 to 12, followed by lunch at the Ritz Hotel. It will be an opportunity for you to meet Tim King, our Managing Director, and the sales team.

We hope you are able to attend the meeting and we look forward to meeting you on April 7.

Yours sincerely

[your full name]

Unit 12   Replies to invitations

Emails

1 Mr Cao and Paul accept the invitation. Ms Schmidt and John cannot accept it.

Understanding

2

1 John
2 Mr Cao
3 Ms Schmidt
4 Paul

Practice

3

Thank you for your invitation to … (F)
Thanks for the invitation to … (I)
XYZ is pleased to accept your invitation (F)
XYZ is free and is looking forward to seeing … . (I)
Unfortunately XYZ is unable to attend … due to … (F)
I'm afraid I can't come because of … . (I)
We wish you success with your event. (F)
I hope everything goes well. (I)

4

1 attend
2 success
3 pleased
4 due
5 free
6 because of

5

1 Thank you for the invitation to the meeting on Friday.
2 We hope everything goes well on Friday.

3 Due to a business trip Ms Goodman is unable to attend.
4 Mr Rogers is pleased to accept your invitation.

6

Suggested answers

1 Thank you for the invitation to your sales conference on September 12.
2 My colleague Jasmine Goodman is pleased to accept.
3 We wish you success with your conference.
4 Yours sincerely

Writing

7

Suggested answers

Accepting the invitation

> Dear Ms Jones
>
> Thank you for your invitation to your company's 25th anniversary. I am pleased to accept your invitation and look forward to seeing you on July 4.
>
> Yours sincerely

Declining (= *not accepting*) the invitation

> Dear Ms Jones
>
> Thank you for your invitation to your company's 25th anniversary. Unfortunately, I am unable to attend due to another appointment.
>
> I wish you success with your event.
>
> Yours sincerely

Unit 13   Incoming calls

Telephone calls

1

A   Alan wants to speak to the Sales Department.

B   Diane can't answer the phone because she is in a meeting.

Understanding

2

1 C   **2** B   **3** B   **4** A

Practice

3

1 C   **2** E   **3** G   **4** B

5 D   **6** A   **7** F

4

1   I'm sorry but Mr Carter's line is busy at the moment.

2   My boss will call back later.

3   I'm afraid he's on a business trip.

4   Can you call back tomorrow morning?

5   I'll put you through to the Sales Department.

5

Suggested answers

1   Can you call back later?

2   I'm afraid she's in a meeting.

3   Can you put me through to the Sales Department?

4   Can you hold, please?

5   I'm afraid she's still engaged.

Speaking

6

Model conversation

Customer	Can I speak to Mr Rogers, please?
You	*I'm afraid Mr Rogers is in a meeting.*
Customer	Oh, I see. Well, can I speak to Pauline Coates in the Sales Department?
You	*I'll put you through.*
Customer	Thanks.
You	*I'm sorry but Ms Coates' line is busy at the moment.*
Customer	Oh, I see.
You	*Can you hold?*
Customer	Hmm, I don't think so.
You	*Can you call back later?*
Customer	Yes, OK, thank you. Bye.
You	*Bye!*

Unit 14   Outgoing calls

Telephone calls

Jasmine only manages to speak to Andrea Schmidt.

Understanding

2

1   No
2   Jasmine wants to check the time of the meeting is OK for Ms Schmidt.
3   Mr Johansson is on a business trip.

Practice

3

1 C	2 A	3 F	4 E
5 B	6 D		

4

1   Can you put me through to James Harris, please?
2   I'm calling about the conference next month.
3   I just want to check your flight number.
4   Can you give me Mr Carter's mobile number?
5   Could I speak to Kate White, please?
6   Well, thanks very much Anthony.

5

[1]	Jasmine	Could I speak to Mr White, please?
[2]	Receptionist	I'll put you through.
[3]	White	Anton White.
[4]	Jasmine	Hi Mr White, this is Jasmine Goodman calling from Lowis Engineering.
[5]	White	Hello, Jasmine.
[6]	Jasmine	I'm just calling about the meeting next Tuesday at 10 o'clock. I just want to check if the time is OK for you.
[7]	White	The time is fine. No problem at all.
[8]	Jasmine	Oh good! Well, thanks a lot Mr White and see you next week.
[9]	White	See you then. Bye.
[10]	Jasmine	Bye.

Speaking

6

Model conversation

Receptionist	Apelles Hotels how can I help you?
You	*Hello this is Mary James from Capital Investments. Can you put me through to Cindy Fox?*
Receptionist	I'll put you through …oh, I'm sorry she's on a business trip.
You	Oh, can you give me her mobile number, please?
Receptionist	Yes, of course. It's 0155 289 6645.
You	*That's 0155 289 6645. Well, many thanks. Goodbye.*
Receptionist	Goodbye.

Answer key / Audio script

Unit 15   When things go wrong

Telephone calls

1

A   A wrong food order.

B   A delivery that has not arrived yet.

Understanding

2

1   False. She did order food from Benji's Catering.

2   True

3   True

4   False. She's waiting for a package she sent to Singapore to be delivered.

5   False. The package is still in Singapore.

6   True

Practice

3

1   D   2   A   3   E   4   B   5   C

4

1   Can you tell me when you will pick up the package?

2   It's concerning our order for office equipment.

3   Something is wrong with the package you delivered.

4   It's concerning my package, tracking number LO 743 KL.

5   What's happened to our delivery?

6   You sent the wrong delivery to our company.

5

Suggested answers

1   Can you tell me when the package will arrive?

2   Can you give me a refund?

3   Could you pick it up?

4   What's happened to our package?

5   You sent a wrong delivery.

Language tip

13 – 30	thirteen – thirty
14 – 40	fourteen – forty
15 – 50	fifteen – fifty
16 – 60	sixteen – sixty
17 – 70	seventeen – seventy
18 – 80	eighteen – eighty
19 – 90	nineteen – ninety

A H J K

B C D E G P T Z (US)

F L M N S X Z (UK)

I Y

O

Q U W

R

Speaking

6

Model conversation

Supplier	Jackson Office Supplies. How can I help you?
You	*This is Cathy King from Apcos Ltd. There's a problem with an order I made last week.*
Supplier	I'm sorry to hear that. Can you give me the order number?
You	*Yes, it's JYG 723 / 19 / BP. You sent the wrong ink for our printers.*

Supplier	Oh, I see.
You	*Could you pick it up and bring the right ink, TP2000?*
Supplier	No problem.
You	*Can you tell me when it'll be delivered?*
Supplier	I think tomorrow should be possible. Is that OK?
You	*That's OK. Thanks very much. Goodbye.*

Unit 16   Telephone messages

Telephone calls
1 Diane is on holiday.

Understanding
2
1 He's flying to London, not Liverpool; next week, not next month.
2 Tina Jones, not James. Meeting on the 14th not the 4th.
3 Mark is emailing something to Diane not sending something in the post.

Practice
3
1 Can I leave a message for Mr Carter?
2 Would you like me to leave him a message?
3 I'll read the message back to you.
4 Could you take a message for Jasmine Goodman?
5 Can I just check the information?
6 Do you want to leave a message for Mr Rogers?

4
Audio script

Jasmine	Jasmine Goodman.
John	Good morning, Jasmine. It's John Carter here.
Jasmine	Hello John, how are you?
John	Fine thanks. Um ... can I speak to Diane?
Jasmine	I'm afraid she's away this week. Would you like me to take a message? Or do you want to send her an email?
John	Actually, could you take a message? I'm driving to the airport at the moment.
Jasmine	No problem.
John	Can you tell her that I want to change the date of our meeting from the 13th to the 30th of this month if that's OK. And I've also changed the restaurant for our lunch. Tell her to meet me at The Anchor Hotel in Mayfair at 1 o'clock. I think she knows the place.
Jasmine	So, I'll read the information back to you: 'John would like to change the date of your meeting from the 13th to the 30th. Please meet him for lunch at The Anchor Hotel in Mayfair at 12 o'clock.'
John	No, 1 o'clock, not 12.
Jasmine	Oops, sorry! 1 o'clock ....

Telephone message
John Carter would like to change the
date of your meeting from the 13th to
the 30th. Please meet him for lunch at
The Anchor Hotel in Mayfair at 1 o'clock.

Speaking

5

Model conversation

Customer	Can I speak to Mr Rogers, please?
You	*I'm afraid Mr Rogers is in a meeting.*
Customer	Oh, I see. I have some some information for him.
You	*Do you want to leave a message for Mr Rogers?*
Customer	Um ... yes, OK. Can you tell him that my conference in June is cancelled. If he wants to speak to me about it, he can call me on my new mobile. The number is 01521 300 9957.
You	*Can I just check the information? The conference in June is cancelled and Mr Rogers can call you on 01521 300 9957.*
Customer	That's right. Thanks very much. Goodbye.
You	*Goodbye.*

Unit 17　Conference arrangements

Telephone call
1　The participants will eat lunch in the hotel restaurant.

Understanding
2
1　True
2　True
3　False. She also wants a flipchart and four pinboards.
4　False. She arranges it for 4.30 pm.
5　True

Practice
3
1　projector　　　4　reserve
2　provide　　　　5　forget
3　mind

4
1　Please could you reserve some tables for us?
2　I'd like to reserve some tickets.
3　Would you mind repeating that back to me, please?
4　Does the room have an Internet connection?
5　Can you organize a meeting for next week?

5
Audio script

Cindy	Apelles Hotel Reservation Department, Cindy Fox speaking. How can I help you?
John	Good morning. My name's John Pitt. I'd like to reserve a room for a meeting from 2 o'clock until 7 o'clock for October 19th.
Cindy	Are you a customer of ours already Mr Pitt?
John	Yes. It's Topaz Lighting.
Cindy	All right. How many participants will there be?
John	15.
Cindy	OK, let me check. Yes, that's fine, Mr Pitt. The Napoleon Suite is available.
John	Excellent, that's fine. Now, does the room include a multimedia projector?
Cindy	Yes, and Internet access. Is there anything else you need?
John	Could you provide a flipchart and DVD player?
Cindy	Yes.
John	Good. Now, can you arrange a coffee break for 4.30, please?
Cindy	OK. What about water and juice during the meeting?
John	Oh, good idea! Next, dinner: Would you reserve tables in the hotel restaurant for 7 o'clock?
Cindy	Certainly, Mr Pitt.
John	Good. Now, would you mind repeating that back to me?

Answer key / Audio script

Cindy	Of course. October 19th, the Napoleon Suite from 2 until 7 for 15 people. Dinner at seven and a coffee break at 4.30 plus water and juice in the meeting room. And you need a multimedia projector, flip chart and DVD player.
John	That's correct.

Customer name: John Pitt

Company: Topaz Lighting

Date: October 19

Time: 2-7 pm

Meeting room: Napoleon Suite

Participant numbers: 15

Equipment required: Multimedia projector, flip chart, DVD player

Refreshments: Coffee break + dinner in hotel restaurant, water and juice for the meeting

Time required: 4.30 coffee, 7.00 dinner

You	*For 14 participants.*
Cindy	Yes, that's fine. The Napoleon Suite is available.
You	*Does the room have an Internet connection?*
Cindy	Yes, it does. Is there anything else you need?
You	*Could you provide a multimedia projector and flip chart?*
Cindy	No problem. What about refreshments?
You	*Can you set up coffee and sandwiches for 12 o'clock, please?*
Cindy	Fine. I'll confirm this is in an email.
You	*Thanks very much. Bye.*

Speaking

6

Model conversation

Cindy	Apelles Hotel Reservation Department, Cindy Fox speaking. How can I help you?
You	*Hello, this is Jasmine Goodman. I'd like to reserve a meeting room for July 30th from 10 o'clock until 3 o'clock.*
Cindy	All, right. For how many participants?

Unit 18   Travel plans

Telephone call

1   Diane will meet Mr Wasilewski on Wednesday afternoon.

Understanding

2

1 C   2 B   3 A

Practice

3

1 C   2 E   3 A   4 D   5 B

4

1   Does 10.30 work for you?
2   Would lunchtime be convenient for you Ms Kennedy?
3   Would it be possible for me to see him tomorrow?
4   Is John available on Monday morning?
5   Could you meet Jasmine at quarter to four?

5

[1]	Jasmine	... Diane will be flying to Warsaw on Monday. Do you have time on Monday?
[2]	Eva	On Monday? Hmm, that's difficult
[3]	Jasmine	Well are you available on Monday evening? Ms Kennedy would like to take you to dinner.
[4]	Eva	That's very kind, but I have another appointment in the evening.
[5]	Jasmine	Mmm, well, would Tuesday morning be convenient for you?
[6]	Eva	Well after 10.00 perhaps.
[7]	Jasmine	Great! How about 11 o'clock? Does that work for you?
[8]	Eva	Sure. That would be fine.

Speaking

6

Model conversation

Customer	So you are flying to Madrid next week? Hmm, when can we meet?
You	*Would it be possible for me to see you on Tuesday?*
Customer	Tuesday? No sorry, I'm away on a business trip.
You	*Are you available on Wednesday morning?*
Customer	I'm afraid Wednesday morning is no good. I have to go to the doctor.
You	*Could you meet on Wednesday afternoon?*
Customer	Um ... yes ... I think so.
You	*Would 3 o'clock be convenient for you?*
Customer	Is a little later possible?
You	*I could meet at 4 o'clock at the latest because I have to leave by 6.00.*
Customer	Yes, that's fine. I'll see you then!

Unit 19 Welcome back

Conversation

1 Paul bought Jasmine a present because she organized their visit to Lowis Engineering and booked them a hotel.

See pages 78–79 for video script.

Understanding

2

1 False. She comes down to meet them in reception.
2 True
3 False. Jasmine makes the hotel reservation for them.
4 True
5 True

Practice

3

1 D   **2** C   **3** B   **4** A

4

1 That's really kind of you.
2 Nice to see you again too, Diane.
3 How are you. Tony?
4 Here's a small present from all of us.
5 Fine, thanks. And how about you?

5

1 to
2 too
3 are
4 thanks
5 well

6 for
7 My
8 this
9 is
10 at

Speaking

6

Model conversation

Colin	Hello! Good to see you again!
You	*Nice to see you again, too, Colin.*
Colin	How are you?
You	*Fine thanks, and you?*
Colin	Very well. And thank you so much for arranging my hotel room.
You	*You're welcome!*
Colin	And here is a small thank you present for all your hard work.
You	*Oh, that's really kind of you!*
Colin	My pleasure!

Unit 20   Plans

Conversation

1 John has already met Jim Gibson before.

See pages 82–83 for video script.

Understanding

2

Today

11.00 am – *arrive Lowis Engineering*
1.00 pm – *tour factory with Diane and Chris Fox*
3.00 pm – *meet engineers*
6.00 pm – *dinner with Diane and Mr Harris*

Tomorrow

9.30 am – *visit test facility. Meet Jim Gibson*
4.00 pm – *taxi from Lowis Engineering to airport*
7.00 pm – *flight to Sydney*

Practice

3

1	first	3	next	5	while
2	after	4	then	6	finally

4

1 Today I'm planning to listen to my English CD while driving to work.
2 First of all, we're having a meeting.
3 After that I'm having lunch with Jasmine.
4 Then I'm writing a report for my boss.
5 Finally, this evening I'm going to a movie.

5

Suggested answers

First of all, on Monday I'm flying to the US to visit our New York office.

After / After that, on Tuesday I'm meeting with the Sales Manager.

And then on Tuesday afternoon I'm having a tour of the warehouse.

Next, on Wednesday I'm having lunch with the Managing Director to discuss the business plan.

Finally, on Friday I'm doing some sightseeing and getting a flight back to London at 10 pm.

Speaking

6

Model conversation

Manager	Ah, there you are. Can you tell me about my schedule for tomorrow with Ms Sahdi?
You	*First of all, at 10 o'clock, you're picking up Ms Sahdi at the airport and showing her the new office.*
Manager	I see. What next?
You	*Next, at 11.00, you're having a meeting with Ms Sahdi and the sales team.*
Manager	Very well. And then?
You	*And then you're taking Ms Sahdi to lunch at 1.00.*
Manager	I see. After that?
You	*After that you're visiting the factory at 3.00 to see the new equipment.*
Manager	Good! Anything else?
You	*Finally, at 7 o'clock, you're going to the theatre and then having dinner.*

Unit 21   A change of plan

Conversation

1   Diane can't come in today because her daughter is sick.

See pages 86–87 for video script.

Understanding

2

Today

11.00 am – *arrive Lowis Engineering*
1.00 pm – *tour test facility*
3.00 pm – *meet Jim Gibson*
6.00 pm – *dinner with Mr Harris*

Tomorrow

9.30 am – *visit factory with Diane and Chris Fox*
4.00 pm – *taxi from Lowis Engineering to airport*
7.00 pm – *flight to Sydney*

Practice

3

1 D   2 A   3 E   4 B   5 C

4

1   The salesteam want to bring forward the telephone conference.
2   I truly apologize for the problems with the hotel.
3   I'm afraid there is a change to the timetable this afternoon.
4   He sent his apologies for the delay.
5   I'm so sorry we put back the presentation to tomorrow.

5

1   afraid (sorry is also possible)
2   sorry
3   truly
4   need
5   up
6   back

Speaking

6

Model conversation

Ms Sahdi	You need to make some changes to the schedule for tomorrow? No problem. Tell me.
You	*I'm so sorry but Mr King is sick, so I'm picking you up at the airport.*
Ms Sahdi	I see.
You	*And I'm bringing forward the visit to the factory to 11 o'clock.*
Ms Sahdi	I see. After that?
You	*I truly apologize but I want to cancel the lunch in the restaurant at 1 o'clock and have sandwiches in the office instead.*
Ms Sahdi	That's fine. I don't eat lunch normally. Any other changes?
You	*I'm moving back the meeting with the sales team to 3 o'clock.*
Ms Sahdi	That's a good idea. And in the evening?
You	*I'm taking you to the theatre and then to dinner.*

Unit 22   How was your visit?

Conversation

1 Paul didn't see the testing equipment.

See pages 90–91 for video script.

Understanding

2
1 B   2 C   3 A

Practice

3
1 I <u>didn't</u> speak to Mr Harris yesterday. He was sick.
2 Jasmine <u>emailed</u> him the report last week.
3 'How long <u>was</u> the flight?' 'It <u>wasn't</u> that long. About two hours.'
4 <u>Did</u> you see Diane this morning?
5 'How long <u>were</u> you in the meeting?' 'I think it <u>was</u> about three hours.'

4
1 How much money did you spend?
2 I checked the equipment last night.
3 Did you email Paul the presentation yesterday?
4 Where did they have lunch?
5 What did Chris Fox show you?

5
1 met
2 did not / didn't go
3 emailed
4 was
5 did, check
6 Were
7 had

Speaking

6
Model conversation

Manager	And can you tell me about this week. What did you do on Monday?
You	*I checked the sales figures.*
Manager	I see. What about the sales presentation?
You	*I went to the sales presentation on Wednesday.*
Manager	How was it?
You	*I thought it was excellent.*
Manager	Very good. And did you visit the customer afterwards?
You	*I visited the customer on Thursday.*
Manager	That's fine. Was Paul Rogers there?
You	*Mr Rogers didn't come to the meeting.*
Manager	That's too bad.
You	*And what did you do this week?*

Unit 23 What can I do for you?

Conversation

1 She does two things for him: prints the draft contract and staples the papers together.

See pages 94–95 for video script.

Understanding

2
1 False
2 False. It is on Paul's flash drive.
3 True
4 True
5 True

Practice

3
1 C   2 E   3 B   4 A   5 D

4
1 Shall we arrange a rental car for you?
2 Would Mr Cao like anything else for his presentation?
3 Can I do anything else for you, John?
4 What can I do for them?
5 Let Jasmine know if you need something.
6 Which file is it?

5

[1]	Jasmine	Sally, can you help me with something?
[2]	Sally	Sure. What can I do for you?
[3]	Jasmine	I need to rent a car for Diane, but I haven't done it before.
[4]	Sally	OK. Well, which type of car does she want?
[5]	Jasmine	Oh, a BMW I think.
[6]	Sally	No problem. Shall I order one for 9 o'clock?
[7]	Jasmine	Yes. 9 o'clock is fine.
[8]	Sally	All right, a BMW. Would you like me to ask them to deliver it to the company?
[9]	Jasmine	Good idea. Then she can get the keys from you.
[10]	Sally	OK. Can I do anything else for you?
[11]	Jasmine	No, that's all. Thanks a lot.
[12]	Sally	You're welcome!

Speaking

6
Model conversation

Manager	Can you help me?
You	*What can I do for you?*
Manager	I need to fly to London on Thursday morning.
You	*Would you like me to book you a flight?*
Manager	Oh, thanks very much. And I need a hotel for Thursday and Friday.
You	*Shall I reserve a room at the Anchor Hotel?*
Manager	Yeah, that's a nice hotel.
You	*Can I do anything else for you?*
Manager	No, that's all at the moment, thanks.
You	*Well, let me know if you need anything else.*

Unit 24   Goodbye

Conversation

1 There is more traffic on the roads on Fridays.

See pages 98-99 for video script.

Understanding

2

1 B   2 A   3 C

Practice

3

1 C   2 E   3 A   4 B   5 D

4

1 Well, goodbye then, Mrs Chen.
2 We hope you enjoyed your stay.
3 We're glad that your visit was interesting.
4 It was great seeing you both again.
5 So, see you again soon, we hope.
6 Goodbye and have a good flight home!

5

1 See you again soon, I hope.
2 I hope you enjoyed the presentation.
3 Have a good flight!
4 Bye, take care!
5 It was nice meeting you again.

Speaking

6

Model conversation

Visitor 1	Well, we must go. Goodbye then.
You	*Goodbye, it was nice meeting you again.*
Visitor 2	Yes, it was. And thanks for making the hotel reservation.
You	*My pleasure. I hope you enjoyed your visit.*
Visitor 1	Oh yes, it was great. I learned a lot.
You	*I'm glad you found your visit useful.*
Visitor 2	Definitely. So see you again soon, I hope.
You	*Yes, I hope so too. Have a good flight. Goodbye.*
Visitor 1	Thanks. Bye.
Visitor 2	Bye bye.
You	*Bye.*

Key phrases for speaking

Dealing with visitors at reception

Good morning / afternoon / evening.
How can I help you?
Can I have your names, please?
I'll call Mr / Mrs / Ms ... .
Can you complete this form, please?
Could you wear this badge, please?
Please take a seat.
Someone will come down to get you.

Meeting company guests

Excuse me, are you ... ?
I'm ... .
This is my colleague, ...
... asked me to meet you.
Welcome to ... .
We need to take the lift / stairs to the 2nd floor.
Come this way, please.
After you.

Asking about and describing responsibilities

What do you do?
Is he / she busy? / Are you busy?
Do you travel with him / her?
I'm a team assistant / PA / receptionist.
I work ... .
I make sure that ... .
I book (hotels / tickets / flights).
I answer the phone.
I reply to emails.
I'm responsible for ... .
I deal with ... .

Polite offers and apologies

Can I take your coats?
Would you like to sit down / have a seat?
Would you like some / a cup of coffee?
Would you like milk and sugar?
What about you ...?
Here you are.
I'm sorry you have to wait, but ... should be here soon.
I'm afraid that ... is (still) in a meeting.

Making small talk

How was your flight / trip / journey?
How is the hotel?
Is this your first time here?
How long are you staying in ...?
What should we do ...?
Do you like (the city)?
Would you like to (sit down)?

Introducing other people

I'd like to introduce ... from ...?
Nice to meet you.
Nice to meet you, too.
Please, call me ... .
This is my colleague, ...
Pleased to meet you.
Pleased to meet you, too.
I see you've met ... already.

Dealing with incoming phone calls

Please hold.
I'll put you through to ... .
I'm sorry but her line's busy at the moment.
Can you hold?
I'm afraid the line's still engaged (UK). / She's / He's still on the line (US).
Can you call back later?
I'm afraid she's not available at the moment.
I'll call back at ... .
(Maybe) speak to you later.

Making phone calls

This is ... calling from ... .
Could I speak to ... , please?
Can you put me through to ... , please?
Hello, I'd like to speak to ... , please.
Can you give me his extension number, please?
I'm calling about ... .
I just want to check ... .

Describing problems and asking for information

There's a problem with ... .
It's concerning ... .
You sent the wrong / a faulty delivery / order.
Something's gone wrong with ... .

Could you collect it / pick it up?
Can you give us a refund?
What's happened to ...?
Can you tell me when it'll be delivered?

Taking and leaving a phone message

Can I take a message?
Do you want to leave a message for her?
Could you take a message?
Can I just check that?
Let me repeat that: ...
I'll read that back to you: ...

Making a reservation for a meeting room

I'd like to book a room for a ... .
Does the room have a ...?
Could you provide a ... and ...?
Can you organize / set up a (coffee break) for ...?
Please could you reserve / book tables in the hotel restaurant?
Would you mind repeating that back to me?
Don't forget the ... .

Asking for an appointment

Would it be possible for her to see you then / on (*Monday*) / at (*2 o'clock*)?
Do you have time on (*Friday*)?
Would (*Monday*) be convenient for you?
Are you / Is she available on (*Thursday*)?
Could you meet (*Diane*) at (*4.30*)?
Does that work for you?

Greeting people you know, giving and receiving a gift

Good to see you again.
Nice to see you again, too!
How are you?
Fine thanks. And you? / How about you?
Very well, thanks.
This is a small present from ... .
Thank you very much! That's really kind of you.

Outlining a schedule

First of all, ...
After / After that, ...
And then ... .
Next ... .
While ... .
Finally, ...

Apologizing

I'm afraid there's a problem.
I truly apologize but ... .
She sends her apologies for ... .
I'd love to ... but ... .
I'm so sorry. / I'm so sorry for (*the mix-up* / *the inconvenience*).

Changing arrangements

We need to adjust the schedule / change the plan.
I want to bring forward (UK) / move up (US) ... .
I want to move / put back ... .

Asking opinions

How was your visit?
What did you think of ...?
Did you like the ...?

Talking about the past

It was ... .
Did you see ...? → Yes, we did. / We saw ... .
How much did it cost? → It cost ... .
I thought it was ... . / I didn't see it.
How long did you stay? → We stayed ... .
I liked it.

Offering help

What can I do for you?
Which document / file / folder is it?
Shall I ...?
Would you like me to ...?
There / Here you are.
Can I do anything else for you?
Let me know if you need anything.

Saying goodbye

Well, goodbye then,
Yes, goodbye. It was nice seeing you again.
Thanks very much for ... .
I hope you enjoyed your visit.
Good. I'm glad it was useful.
So, see you again soon, I hope.
Bye, bye. Take care.
Bye. Have a good flight!

Key phrases for writing

Asking for information

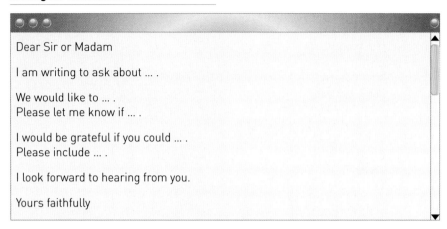

Dear Sir or Madam

I am writing to ask about ... .

We would like to ... .
Please let me know if ... .

I would be grateful if you could ... .
Please include ... .

I look forward to hearing from you.

Yours faithfully

Giving information

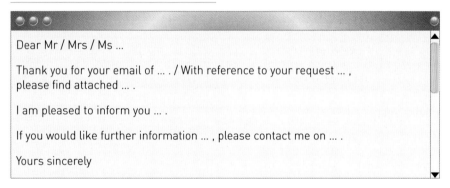

Dear Mr / Mrs / Ms ...

Thank you for your email of ... . / With reference to your request ... ,
please find attached ... .

I am pleased to inform you ... .

If you would like further information ... , please contact me on ... .

Yours sincerely

Asking for help

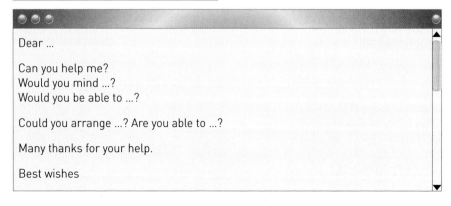

Dear ...

Can you help me?
Would you mind ...?
Would you be able to ...?

Could you arrange ...? Are you able to ...?

Many thanks for your help.

Best wishes

Making suggestions and offering help

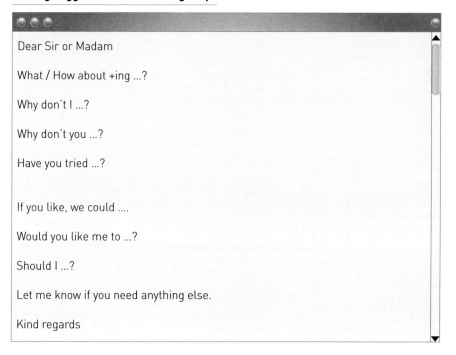

Dear Sir or Madam

What / How about +ing ...?

Why don't I ...?

Why don't you ...?

Have you tried ...?

If you like, we could ....

Would you like me to ...?

Should I ...?

Let me know if you need anything else.

Kind regards

Invitations

Formal

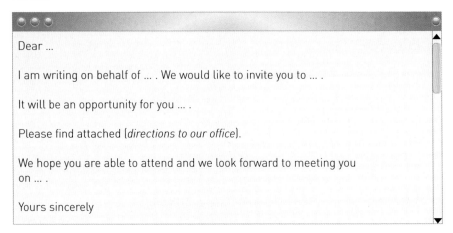

Dear ...

I am writing on behalf of ... . We would like to invite you to ... .

It will be an opportunity for you ... .

Please find attached (*directions to our office*).

We hope you are able to attend and we look forward to meeting you on ... .

Yours sincerely

Informal

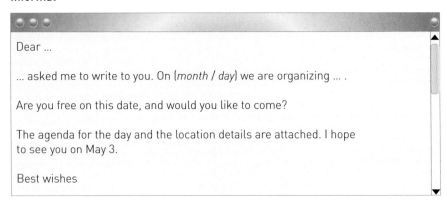

Dear ...

... asked me to write to you. On (*month / day*) we are organizing ... .

Are you free on this date, and would you like to come?

The agenda for the day and the location details are attached. I hope to see you on May 3.

Best wishes

Replying to invitations

Formal

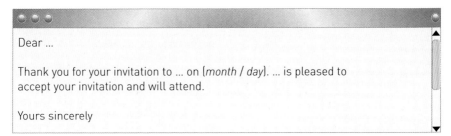

Dear ...

Thank you for your invitation to ... on (*month / day*). ... is pleased to accept your invitation and will attend.

Yours sincerely

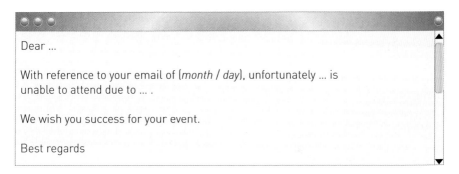

Dear ...

With reference to your email of (*month / day*), unfortunately ... is unable to attend due to ... .

We wish you success for your event.

Best regards

Informal

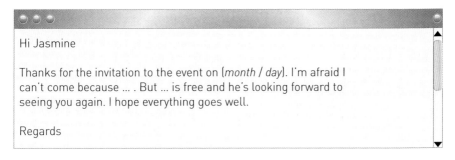

Hi Jasmine

Thanks for the invitation to the event on (*month / day*). I'm afraid I can't come because ... . But ... is free and he's looking forward to seeing you again. I hope everything goes well.

Regards

The standard way to address an envelope in the UK is:

Mr / Mrs / Ms A Brown	*name of recipient*
Lowis Engineering PLC	*name of recipient's company or organization*
Lowis House	*name of building – where applicable*
21 Wardour Street	*building number and street name*
London	*city or town*
W1 0TH	*postcode*
United Kingdom	*country*

The standard way to address an envelope in the US is:

Jonathan Brown	*name of recipient*
Lowis Engineering	*name of recipient's company or organization*
10 East 53rd Street	*building number and street name*
New York NY 10022	*city, state, zip code*

But other countries do it differently. In Japan, for example, the name of the recipient is put at the bottom of the address. In France, the whole address should be in CAPITAL LETTERS, except the name of the recipient. Use the Internet to check how to write different international addresses.

Email signatures

Some companies have standard email signatures. This is Jasmine's:

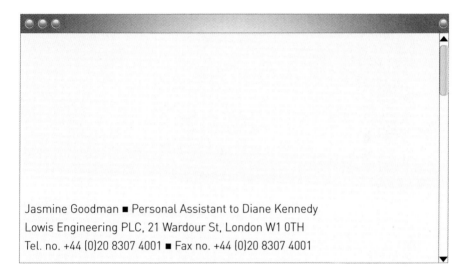

Jasmine Goodman ■ Personal Assistant to Diane Kennedy
Lowis Engineering PLC, 21 Wardour St, London W1 0TH
Tel. no. +44 (0)20 8307 4001 ■ Fax no. +44 (0)20 8307 4001

Out-of-office messages

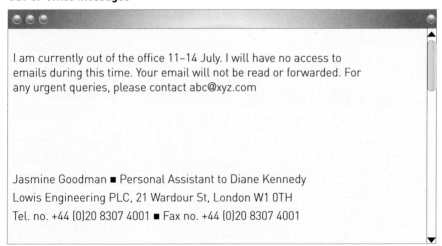

I am currently out of the office 11–14 July. I will have no access to emails during this time. Your email will not be read or forwarded. For any urgent queries, please contact abc@xyz.com

Jasmine Goodman ■ Personal Assistant to Diane Kennedy
Lowis Engineering PLC, 21 Wardour St, London W1 0TH
Tel. no. +44 (0)20 8307 4001 ■ Fax no. +44 (0)20 8307 4001

Lowis Engineering

Schedule:
John Carter and Paul Rogers, Australian Power Utilities

Tuesday 15th November

1.30–3.30	Tour of factory
	with Chris Fox (Factory Manager) and Diane Kennedy
3.30–5.00	Discussion of ideas for new equipment
	with Diane Kennedy and the team of engineers
6.30 onwards	Dinner
	with Mr Harris (Managing Director) and Diane Kennedy

Wednesday 16th November

9.30	Pick-up from hotel to go to test facility
	with Diane Kennedy and Jasmine Goodman
10.00–3.00	Test facility tour
	with Jim Gibson (Test Manager)
4.00	Pick-up from office to airport
7.00	Flight departs to Australia

Minutes of the meeting

Date: June 27, 2011.
Time: 3.30-5.30
Place: Boardroom 3
Meeting objective: Diane Kennedy's visit to APU August 7-11
Present: Lowis Engineering: Dianne Kennedy (DK), Jasmine Goodman (JG),
Australian Power Utilities: John Carter (JC), Paul Rogers (PR)
Apologies: Lowis Engineering: Jennifer Williams (JW)

Points discussed

1. Trip schedule
DK to meet the APU Managing Director in Perth.
PR to confirm the trip to the APU Head Office in Sydney.
PR to send a schedule for the trip by August 1.

2. Travel arrangements
PR to arrange accommodation for DK.
JG to be responsible for travel arrangements.

3. AOB
JC to send the marketing plan by July 10.
DK to send feedback on the marketing plan by July 30.

Did you know?

In minutes we usually use the form *X to do something.*

Key words

Companies

	Your translation
boss	
branch	
colleague	
department	
division	
employee	
employer	
headquarters	
job	
to manage	

Computers

	Your translation
bug	
computer	
crash	
document	
drop-down menu	
error	
file	
keyboard	
LAN	
laptop	
monitor	
mouse	
patch	
password	
printer	
printer cartridge	
program	
pop-up	
software	
tablet	
virus	
Wi-Fi	
to delete	
to log off	
to log on	
to save	

Deliveries	
	Your translation
address	
lorry (UK) / truck (US)	
package	
parcel	
registered post	
special delivery	
tracking number	
truck (US) / lorry (UK)	
to delay	
to deliver	
to order	
to post	
to send	

Departments	
	Your translation
Accounting	
Customer Services	
Distribution	
Human Resources	
Information Technology (IT)	
Logistics	
Marketing	
Payroll	
Production	
Research and Development	
Sales	
Security	
Transport	
Warehousing	

Key words

Events and meetings	
	Your translation
catering	
change	
conference room	
equipment	
event	
facilities	
flipchart	
invitation	
meeting room	
participant	
presentation	
projector	
to arrange	
to attend	
to book	
to bring forward	
to cancel	
to invite	
to organize	
to put / move back	
to reserve	

Industry	
	Your translation
advertising	
automotive / car	
aviation	
banking	
catering	
construction	
consumer electronics	
energy	
fashion	
food and drink	
healthcare	
insurance	
logistics	
telecommunications	
tourism	
pharmaceuticals	
public relations	
publishing	
retail	
waste disposal / management	
water	

In the office	
	Your translation
chair	
computer	
cubicle / work station	
desk	
fax machine	
hole punch (UK) / hole puncher (US)	
paper	
paper clip	
pen	
pencil	
photocopy (UK) / Xerox (US)	
print out	
stapler	
stationery	
telephone	
Xerox (US) / photocopy (UK)	
to fax	
to photocopy (UK) / to Xerox (US)	
to print something out	
to staple	
to Xerox (US) / to photocopy (UK)	

Office job titles	
	Your translation
chairman / chairwoman	
chief executive officer	
chief financial officer	
clerk	
consultant	
engineer	
lawyer	
manager	
managing director	
personal assistant	
receptionist	
salesman / saleswoman / salesperson	
secretary	

Projects	
	Your translation
budget	
client	
cost	
deadline	
delivery	
goal	
plan	
phase	
project	
project manager / member / team	
quality	
resources	
schedule	
status	
time	

Key words

Reception	
	Your translation
appointment	
badge	
desk	
elevator (US) / lift (UK)	
entrance	
foyer	
guest	
lift (UK) / elevator (US)	
seat	
security	
visitor	

Refreshments	
	Your translation
biscuit (UK) / cookie (US)	
coffee	
cup	
glass	
juice	
milk	
mineral water	
sandwich	
sugar	
tea	

Telephone	
	Your translation
busy (line)	
cell (US) / mobile (UK) phone	
engaged (line) (UK)	
extension	
line	
mobile (UK) phone / cell (US)	
to call	
to call back	
to connect *someone to someone*	
to hold (*the line*)	
to put *someone* through *to someone*	
to ring	

Travel	
	Your translation
flight	
hire car / car rental	
journey	
plane	
subway (US) / underground (UK)	
taxi	
tour	
traffic	
train	
trip	
underground (UK) / subway (US)	

Present simple

Positive forms:	I **work** on the reception desk.
	She **enjoys** her job very much.
	Our employees **love** helping visitors.
Negative forms:	I **don't [do not] work** for Lowis Engineering.
	This visitor **doesn't [does not] have** a security card.
	We **don't allow** pets in the company.
Questions:	**Does** she **work** for Lowis Engineering?
	Where **do** you **come** from?
Long answers:	Yes, she **does work** for Lowis Engineering.
	No, she **doesn't work** for Lowis Engineering.
Short answers:	Yes, I **do**.
	No, I **don't**.
	Yes, she **does**.
	No, she **doesn't**.

This tense is used to express facts:

- Jasmine **works** at Lowis Engineering in London but she **lives** in Wimbledon.
- The office **is** on the corner of Wardour Street and Oxford Street.
- Diane **works** in London but she **comes** from Ireland.

and for actions that are regular activities or routines:

- I **check** my emails every day.
- The postman **brings** the post before lunch.

It is also used in with timetables and schedules:

- The canteen **opens** at 12 o'clock.
- The company **closes** at midnight.

It is also used in clauses with *if, when, until, as soon as* **and** *after*:

- She'll give you her address *when* she **telephones**.
- I'll help you *after* I **finish** this report.
- We'll start the meeting *as soon as* the boss **arrives**.
- Let's wait *until* Paul **gets here**.

Words that often take the present simple are: *often, seldom, usually, never, always, normally, rarely*:

- It **often** rains a lot in April.
- We **never** close.

Present continuous

Positive form:	I'm [I am] **waiting** for my taxi.
	We're [We are] **staying** in the Anchor Hotel.
	They're [They are] **having** a meeting.
Negative form:	No, I'm **not staying** in the country.
	She **isn't** [She **is not**] **waiting** for Diane.
Questions:	**Are** you **staying** at the Anchor Hotel?
	Is Mr Jones **waiting** to see me?
	When **are** they **leaving**?
Long answers:	Yes. I'm **staying** at the Anchor.
	No, I'm **not** staying in London.
Short answers:	Yes, I **am**.
	Yes, she **is**.
	Yes, they **are**.
	No, I'm **not**.
	No, she **isn't**.
	No, they **aren't**.

This tense is used to describe an action that is happening NOW:

- Would you like an umbrella because it's **raining** (now)?

Or an action that has started but is not finished:

- I'm **waiting** to see him.

It is also used for temporary actions or situations:

- She's **staying** at the Anchor Hotel in London for three nights.

It can also have a future meaning and is used to talk about future activities that have been arranged or planned:

- I'm **staying** in the hotel next week too.

Words that often take the present continuous are: *now, at the moment, presently.*

Watch out – we don't usually use these verbs in the continuous form:

> remember, understand, want, like, belong, suppose, need, seem, prefer, believe, know, think (= believe), hear, smell, have (= possess)

Past simple

Positive form:	He **arrived** yesterday.
	I **confirmed** my meeting last week.
	We **visited** the company last month.
	She **knew** there was a delay.
	We **ate** in the restaurant last night.
Negative form:	He **didn't** [**did not**] **telephone** yesterday.
	You **didn't tell** me that I would have to pay.
	They **didn't enjoy** their visit.
	I **didn't expect** to have to wait so long at reception.
Questions:	**Did** Mr Lawson **arrive** yesterday?
	Did you **enjoy** your visit?
	Did the suppliers **receive** their money?
	What **did** you **buy** in London?
Long answers:	Yes, he **arrived** yesterday.
	No, he **didn't arrive** yesterday.
	Yes, we **spoke** to the manager about your problem.
	No, we **didn't speak** to the manager about your problem.
Short answers:	Yes, we **did**.
	No, we **didn't**.
	Yes, I **did**.
	No, I **didn't**.

This tense is used for finished actions in the past:

- I **visited** your company last week.

and for longer situations in the past:

- I **worked** at Siemens for 20 years.

Words that often take the past simple are: *yesterday, an hour ago, last year, in 2009, last week, a year ago.*

Going to future

Positive form:	I'm [I am] **going to send** an email tomorrow.
	They're [They **are**] **going to complain** about the meeting.
	He's [He **is**] **going to book** three conference rooms.
	We're **going to write** to the manager.
Negative form:	I'm not [I am not] **going to telephone** tomorrow.
	We **aren't** [We **are not**] **going to eat** in the restaurant tonight.
	She **isn't going to go** to Australia.
Questions:	**Are** you **going to telephone** tomorrow?
	Is he **going to tell** the boss?
	Who's **going to tell** the boss?
Long answers:	Yes, I'm **going to telephone** tomorrow.
	No, I'm **not going to telephone** tomorrow.
	Yes, they're **going to email** the manager.
	No, they **aren't going to email** the manager.
Short answers:	Yes, I **am**.
	No, I'm **not**.
	Yes, he **is**.
	No, he **isn't**.
	Yes, they **are**.
	No, they **aren't**.

This tense is used to say something has been planned or decided and will definitely happen:

- We're **going to move** offices next year.
- When **are** you **going to get** a company car?
- When I get home, I'm **going to write** a report about the conference.

Simple future – will

Positive form:	I'll [I will] **post** it tomorrow. We'll **arrange** a meeting. Sally'll **call** me as soon as your taxi is here.
Negative form:	I **won't** [will not] **do** it tomorrow. Jasmine **won't forget** to do it, Paul. They **won't come** back.
Questions:	**Will** you **do** it tomorrow? **Will** she **order** me a taxi? When **will** my taxi **come**?
Long answers:	Yes, I'**ll do** it in a minute. No, I **won't do** it today.
Short answers:	Yes, I will. No, I won't.

This tense is used for predictions about the future:

- In the year 2020 we'**ll** all **work** until we are 75.
- You'**ll** never **finish** that report before 1.00.

It is also used to give information about the future (that does <u>not</u> involve intentions or arrangements):

- In ten minutes we'**ll test** the fire alarm.

It must also be used for conditional use, for example in *if*-sentences:

- If you do not cancel in time, you'**ll have to** pay a fee.

It is also used to announce a decision in offers, promises and threats, requests and instructions, and suggestions:

- That sounds good. I'**ll have** the steak too.
- I'**ll tell** you as soon as the report is ready.
- I promise I'**ll** inform my boss immediately.
- Do that again and I'**ll complain** your boss.
- **Will** you **fill** in this form, please?

Present perfect simple

Positive form:	I've [I have] **worked here** for ten years. She's [She has] **done** secretarial work for ten years. The manager **has read** your letter.
Negative form:	I **haven't [have not] worked** in an office before. She **hasn't [has not] ordered** a taxi.
Questions:	**Have** you **worked** in London before? **Has** my taxi **been** ordered? Where **have** you **put** the brochures?
Long answers:	Yes, I**'ve worked** in London for five years. No, I **haven't [have not] ordered** a taxi.
Short answers:	Yes, I **have**. No, I **haven't**. Yes, it **has**. No, it **hasn't**.

This tense is used to describe a completed action in the past which is still relevant to the present:

- Can you help me? I**'ve lost** the key to my office. (= I don't have it.)
- We have to cancel our visit because she's **broken** her leg. (= Her leg is broken.)
- I**'ve read** some information about your company. (= I know about the company.)
- We**'ve moved** offices since your last visit. (= The offices are different.)

> Note that we do not use the present perfect if we say when something happened, for example, with finished time expressions such as yesterday, last week, at 10 o'clock this morning, in 2010, last October.

- I'm sure we**'ve met** before!
- **Have** you ever **stayed** in the Anchor Hotel before?
- My boss **has been** to a conference here.
- The hotel **has been** in the Anchor Group for over 25 years.

It is also used to describe events with expressions of 'time elapsing up to now'. Signal words are *just, yet, already.*

- **Have you sent** the report **yet**?
- She's **just finished** the email.
- We've **just received** a phone call from Paul Rogers.
- I've **already ordered** Mrs Wilson's coffee.

Irregular verbs

Infinitive	Past simple	Past participle	Infinitive	Past simple	Past participle
be	was	been	meet	met	met
become	became	become	pay	paid	paid
blow	blew	blown	put	put	put
break	broke	broken	read	read	read
bring	brought	brought	ring	rang	rung
build	built	built	rise	rose	risen
buy	bought	bought	ran	run	ran
choose	chose	chosen	say	said	said
come	came	come	see	saw	seen
cost	cost	cost	sell	sold	sold
cut	cut	cut	send	sent	sent
do	did	done	show	showed	shown
drink	drank	drunk	shut	shut	shut
drive	drove	driven	sit	sat	sat
eat	ate	eaten	speak	spoke	spoken
fall	fell	fallen	spend	spent	spent
find	found	found	stand	stood	stood
fly	flew	flown	steal	stole	stolen
get	got	got / gotten (US)	stick	stuck	stuck
give	gave	given	swim	swam	swum
have	had	had	take	took	taken
hear	heard	heard	teach	taught	taught
hide	hid	hidden	tell	told	told
hold	held	held	think	thought	thought
keep	kept	kept	understand	understood	understood
know	knew	known	wear	wore	worn
lead	led	led	win	won	won
learn	learned	learned	write	wrote	written
leave	left	left			
lend	lent	lent			
let	let	let			
make	made	made			
mean	meant	meant			

a/c	account
am	to show the time is between midnight and noon
AGM	annual general meeting
AOB	any other business
approx	approximately
asap	as soon as possible
bcc	blind copied to
cc	copied to
CEO	chief executive officer
FAO	for the attention of
FAQ	frequently asked question
Inc	incorporated
Ltd	limited
N/A	not applicable
NB	pay particular attention to this
PA	personal assistant
p.a.	per annum (per year)
pm	to show the time is between noon and midnight
PR	public relations
PTO	please turn over
p.w.	per week
qty	quantity
R&D	research and development
re	with reference to
RSVP	please reply (French: répondez s'il vous plaît)
VAT	value added tax
WWW	world wide web

Dates	
You write	**You say**
Monday 18 August (especially UK)	Monday, the eighteenth of August
Monday, August 18 (US)	Monday, August (the) eighteenth
2011	two thousand and eleven *OR* twenty eleven
2/11/2011 (UK)	the second of November, two thousand and eleven *OR* twenty eleven
11/2/2011 (US)	November the second, two thousand and eleven *OR* twenty eleven
October 3rd (US)	October (the) third
3rd October (UK)	the third of October

- In British English you usually write and say dates like this: date / month / year.
- In American English you usually write and say dates like this: month / date / year.

Times	
The time is....	**You say**
09.15	nine fifteen *OR* quarter past nine *OR* quarter after nine (US)
10.00	ten o'clock (in the morning) *OR* ten am
22.00 (UK)	ten o'clock (in the evening) *OR* ten pm
11.30	eleven thirty *OR* half past eleven
14.40	fourteen forty (UK) *OR* two forty in the afternoon *OR* twenty to three
16.20	sixteen twenty *OR* twenty past four (in the afternoon) *OR* twenty after four (US)
16.21	sixteen twenty one *OR* twenty one minutes past four
15.00	fifteen hundred (hours) *OR* three o'clock (in the afternoon)
17.45	seventeen forty-five *OR* quarter to six

- In American English you don't use the 24-hour clock. For example, 22.00 is 10 pm and 10.00 is 10 am.

Time	
1.5 hours	ninety minutes *OR* one and a half hours *OR* an hour and a half
15 minutes	fifteen minutes *OR* quarter of an hour
30 minutes	thirty minutes *OR* half an hour
45 minutes	forty five minutes *OR* three quarters of an hour

- In British English you use the 24-hour clock (16.45 = sixteen forty five) mainly to talk about train and flight times. The 24-hour clock is rarely used in American English.
- We don't usually use the 24-hour clock (16.45 = sixteen forty five) in everyday language. For example, we do not say *The meeting will start at fifteen hundred hours* but we do say *The meeting will start at three pm / at three o'clock.*

Prices	
You write	You say
£10.99	ten pounds ninety-nine (pence)
€140.00	one hundred (and) forty euros
$22.90	twenty-two (dollars) (and) ninety (cents)
£87.00	eighty-seven pounds

Telephone numbers	
The telephone number is:	You say:
0044 171 200 3612	double oh, double four, one seven one, two double oh, three six one two (UK)
0044 171 200 3612	zero zero four four, one seven one, two zero zero, three six one two (US)
020 677 3219	oh two oh six double seven, three two one nine
ex: 5640	extension five six four oh (UK)
ex: 5640	extension five six four zero / oh (US)

- In American English you don't usually say double four or treble four. Just say four four, or four, four, four.
- You can say *oh* or *zero* for the number 0. *Zero* is used more often in American English.

Email addresses and websites	
The email address is:	You say:
jasmine.goodman@lowis.com	jasmine dot goodman at Lowis dot com
The website address is:	You say:
www.lowisengineering.com/aboutus	www dot lowis engineering dot com forward slash about us

You can use these phrases when you're on the phone. Why don't you photocopy these 2 pages and keep them near the telephone for easy reference?

52 CD

Asking to speak to someone on the phone

- Could I speak to _____, please?
- Can I speak to _____, please?
- Could you put me through to _____, please?
- I'm trying to contact _____.
- I'm trying to get in touch with _____.
- I'm trying to get hold of _____.

Asking for identification on the phone

- Who's calling, please?
- Who's speaking?
- Who shall I say is calling?
- Could I have your name (again), please?
- Could you give me your name, please?
- I'm sorry I didn't quite catch / get your name.
- Would you mind spelling that (your name / first name / surname) for me?
- Could you spell that for me?

Asking for repetition / clarification on the phone

- I'm sorry, I didn't quite catch / get that. Could you repeat it?
- I'm afraid that was a little (bit) too fast. Would you mind repeating it more slowly for me?
- I didn't understand the last word of the address. Could you give it to me again?
- Is that Mr Smith or Mrs?
- I'm sorry, did you say Oxford Road or Oxford Parade?
- I beg your pardon? / Pardon?
- Sorry?
- I'm (very) sorry. I'm not familiar with English / French / Japanese surnames. Could you spell that for me?
- Could you repeat that a little more slowly, please?

 You may photocopy these pages.

Asking the caller to wait

- Hold the line, please.
- Please hold the line.
- Would you (just) hold the line a moment, please?
- (Just) One moment, please. I'm just putting you through to that room / department.
- Could you hold on a moment, please?
- Could you wait a moment, please?
- One moment, please. I'll be with you in a second.

Answering the phone

- Good morning, Lowis Engineering. Simon speaking. How can I help you?
- Good morning, Lowis Engineering. Simon speaking. How may I direct your call?

Offering to help

- I'm sorry, the line's busy. Can I help?
- I'm sorry, there's no one answering. Can I take a message?
- Would you like to leave a message?

The aviation alphabet

Use the following words to check spelling.

My name's Mr Whyte – that's W for Whisky, H for Hotel, Y for Yankee, T for Tango and E for Echo.

A for Alpha	G for Golf	M for Mike	S for Sierra	Y for Yankee
B for Bravo	H for Hotel	N for November	T for Tango	Z for Zulu
C for Charlie	I for India	O for Oscar	U for Uniform	
D for Delta	J for Juliet	P for Papa	V for Victor	
E for Echo	K for Kilo	Q for Quebec	W for Whisky	
F for Foxtrot	L for Lima	R for Romeo	X for X-Ray	

Note that Z is pronounced *zee* in American English and *zed* in British English.